338

D1186656

Trading in Options

An investor's guide to making high profits
in the traded options market

GEOFFREY CHAMBERLAIN

SECOND EDITION

WOODHEAD-FAULKNER · CAMBRIDGE

Published by Woodhead-Faulkner Limited
Fitzwilliam House, 32 Trumpington Street
Cambridge CB2 1QY, England
and
51 Washington Street
Dover, NH 03820, USA

First published 1981
Second edition 1982
Second impression 1983
Third impression 1986
Fourth impression 1986

ISBN 0 85941 218 0

Typeset by Rowland Phototypesetting Limited
Bury St Edmunds, Suffolk

Printed in Great Britain by
St Edmundsbury Press Limited
Bury St Edmunds, Suffolk

Preface

The prime objective of this book is to introduce the new, exciting world of traded options to the multitude of investors in Europe who have yet to discover one of the fastest-growing and most flexible investment media available. The book has been written for any and every serious investor or manager of money, whether private or institutional, male or female, young or old, conservative or bold in outlook, disillusioned or starry-eyed with the performance of his (or her) equity portfolio over the years. Indeed, traded options have something positive to offer anyone, at any level of expertise, who feels the need for an investment medium which purports to be of real assistance in modifying the risks inherent in equity investment and who is prepared to research and investigate the subject properly and *without prejudice*. That is all I ask. Those who are prepared to do this have a real treat in store – they will never regret the experience – while those who master it and use it intelligently to augment a declared investment strategy will be rewarded handsomely. What is more, they will enjoy it: for the vast majority of private investors, enjoyment and investment in equities have not often walked hand in hand for many years.

Of course, successful investment in equities is not, never has been and never will be a wholly rational activity; nor is it easy, no matter what the so-called experts imply! Growing pressures on fund managers to perform creditably have tended to intensify the already extreme volatility of price movement over historically short time scales. Thus, the 'natural' inclination among investors to seek the comparative comfort of the herd as it chases ever-shortening trends more often than not these days results in exaggerated swings out of all proportion to the volume of business transacted, and produces a widening disparity of 'sector performance' as the race to find the new growth areas accelerates. More than at any time since I entered the Exchange in the early 1960s, we now have a 'market in stocks' as distinct from a 'stock market'.

The sheer speed and magnitude of today's price volatility renders the task of reading violent short-term trends a most difficult and potentially hazardous occupation, particularly for the private investor. Against a background of the *staccato* stop/go economic policies (for want of a better phrase) of successive governments, the decade of the 1970s witnessed a steady exodus of private investor interest in equities as a formidable combination of high inflation, high dealing costs, poor profitability and inadequate return on capital employed took its toll. The gradual withdrawal of the disillusioned private investor and the increasing dominance of the institutional funds is a sad development which has been one-way for far too long.

It is not difficult to see why. It is not easy to be a 'winner' in a market environment that is essentially bullish in make-up but hosts a list of 30 leading shares in the Financial Times Index that have broken through the 500 level no less than 33 times since 1970, not only failing to sustain the level on each occasion but dropping as low as 146 in the process. On each occasion above this level, equity volume swelled as the ever-hopeful private investor returned to the fray, only to be disappointed yet again. High and continuing inflation severely dented capital committed heavily to equities over the decade, while the incidence of a penal, inequitable tax burden on dividend income (for much of this period) left the return on capital employed inadequate and somewhat pitiful.

However, it would be unrealistic to imagine that a traded options market will necessarily arrest this trend or solve but a small proportion of the problems. For one thing, the market will always be limited (relative to the whole) to a small number of underlying shares. This should not be dismissed out of hand though: while only 18 shares list options in London at the time of writing, they nevertheless account for a significant percentage of its total market capitalisation. This is not too bad for 'starters' since the numbers will undoubtedly grow as the medium gains acceptance and use.

Traded options do not offer any magical solutions but they do have an important role to play in modern portfolio management. It is my hope that, as the chapters of the book unfold, it will become increasingly clear that traded options have a great deal to offer virtually every investor involved in equities. Indeed, anyone who is convinced that he (or she) can disregard the immense flexibility of action that the medium permits or the investment 'insurance' policies it offers is most fortunate. I need all the help I can get and welcome it gratefully!

For the beginner (as indeed the vast majority of investors in Europe must be), the early chapters trace the history of options, introducing the concept and the structure, and include some of the basic terms and definitions. The progression from this point should be rapid. The budding option trader should find enough substance and strategic guidance in the chapter devoted to purchasing options to accommodate most of his aspirations in this sphere. The writer (seller) of options, whether covered (by a position in the underlying security) or uncovered, will find much to digest in this section of the text. If the book enables but a small number of writers to augment the return on their equity portfolio or improve the performance through greater flexibility (as should be possible through use of the medium), then much will have been achieved.

In between the straightforward buying and selling of traded options there lies a vast area of more sophisticated option strategies, tailor-made to accommodate the multitude of investment views likely to materialise at any time. The permutations and combinations available are virtually unlimited; the investor with an agile, flexible mind will have a field-day. However, as I advise later, the advanced strategies should be treated with caution until some general expertise has been acquired.

The important subject of the taxation treatment of traded options has been covered in detail. It has taken almost three years to achieve the fiscal amendments now relevant; I wish no one to be under any misapprehension concerning the former problems or the present position.

Put options on just three classes were introduced on the London Traded Options Market in May 1981: by the end of the year the number had increased to ten. At the time of writing, put options are traded on eleven classes, and a listing for the outstanding seven classes remains a high priority. Logically, whenever new classes are introduced, puts and calls should be listed simultaneously. The subject of put options is an extremely important one, not only to provide both buyer and writer with the same gearing and flexibility available to their call option counterparts, but also to extend considerably the scope for combining the two and thus effecting some of the more varied and sophisticated strategies.

The book is designed to provide a practical manual for option traders. A mastery of the concept and techniques described, and adherence to the 'rules' advocated will leave the reader eager to start and well equipped to do so. However, before acting too precipitously, it would be advisable to seek expert assistance from one of the few specialist brokers in London.   G.H.C.

Contents

1

History and introduction

New options are always suspected and usually opposed, without any other reason but because they are not already common.   *Anon.*

BACKGROUND

The earliest use of the concept of an option contract can be traced to the Middle Ages, when it was used simply and constructively to augment the normal flow of trade and commerce. As the centuries rolled on, the basic concept was occasionally extended, manipulated, and packaged with the requisite ingredients of financial sophistication and speculative 'mystique' tailored to appeal greatly to the natural avarice of mere mortals. While this appeal was strong, the underlying structure lacked foresight, adequate controls and the liquidity necessary to provide the solid foundations upon which to build. As a result, many ill-conceived, manipulative ploys masking behind the concept of an option led to much abuse and financial misdemeanour. As early as the seventeenth century the speculative use of options in the tulip bulb débâcle in Holland (which subsequently led to a collapse in the entire Dutch economy) did little to enhance the reputation of or confidence in the medium. The multitude of manipulative option schemes which mushroomed in the 1920s, particularly in America, continued to leave a bitter taste in the mouths of those who, by either their association with or participation in such schemes, suffered loss of capital, personal pride or both. Whether strictly accurate or not was hardly the point; options were held to be the villain of the piece!

As a result, although puts and calls have been traded on securities in

London since the end of the seventeenth century, they have been treated very much as a peripheral activity by the financial community, and tarnished with the speculative image that is normally the running-mate of a somewhat unpleasant background. The history of the Inland Revenue's mistrust of options (which has caused some of us a great deal of aggravation over the past four years) dates from the early 1960s, when a number of ingenious tax-avoidance schemes were set up involving the creation of purely fictitious options. And so it goes on!

It is perhaps not unreasonable to suggest that more might have and should have been done by the advocates of and participants in the traditional option market, mainly to counter some of the unfair, unreasonable and, above all, inaccurate charges that were levelled at the subject matter *ad nauseam* over the years. No serious, sustained attempt was made to educate the financial community with first class literature or stylish presentations highlighting the advantages that options offered in money management. As a result, it would have been foolhardy to expect anything other than apathy from the passive majority and a mountain of criticism bordering on sheer hostility from a vociferous minority towards the foetal traded options market: many hoped it would abort or at best be still-born. Indeed, for a 'peripheral' financial activity I was amazed at the weight and intensity of the opposition to it which grew to a crescendo early in 1978 in London, when the concept threatened to become an actuality despite the extraordinary volume growth in activity achieved by the Chicago Board Options Exchange (CBOE) since 1973 in America.

As I have already said, much of the early criticism was negative and ill-informed, but not all. Despite the fact that many people laboured (and still do) under a number of general misconceptions, three basic questions were consistently raised in considering the establishment of a market in traded options. These questions, namely what is such a market about, who is it for and how relevant is it, had validity and deserved an answer. In a speech early in 1979 J. P. Clay, one of the 'early' Stock Exchange advocates of the establishment of a traded options market in Europe, answered these three questions as follows.

The answer to the first question is really quite simple: the market is concerned with risk management. It is a common experience of investors, both private and institutional, that it is difficult for them to adjust the overall exposure to risk of their portfolios (what the theoreticians call risk variability, or beta) in order to take account of short- and medium-term expectations of market movement without undertaking large programmes of

2

either borrowing for the purpose of purchase or realisation into cash. A programme of this kind disturbs the long-term balance of the portfolio, may well disrupt materially the pattern of income flow and certainly involves large transaction costs. Where a market in traded options exists, those who are managing portfolios can choose either to increase or to reduce their exposure to risk with minimal disturbance to the basic portfolio and at modest cost.

It follows from this that the market is designed for both private and institutional investors. Many commentators have assumed that the former will be buyers and the latter sellers, but this is an unduly simplistic view of the way the market actually works. In practice it is probably more accurate to assume that among private investors the younger ones will be buyers and the older will be sellers, because the former are more able to accept risk and the latter are happy to increase their income and simultaneously reduce the degree of fluctuation in their portfolio, but even this simplification is not necessarily true. Retired investors, for example, may find in certain circumstances that their preferences are best expressed by a combination of fixed-interest securities and long positions in options. The fact of the matter is that the increased flexibility represented by the existence of traded options can be of benefit in one way or another to every investor, and generalisations about the way in which any type of investor will best be able to get the benefit should be treated with caution.

The third question, that is the importance of the market, follows on naturally from the above. It has, however, been confused by exaggerations propounded both by supporters and by opponents of traded options. The former have put forward unrealistically optimistic assessments of the benefits that could realistically be expected, while the latter have almost suggested that the whole idea was the invention of the devil. I think that it is more reasonable to say that, in our belief, a market in traded options is a modest but useful addition to the range of choice available to investors, and that this is quite sufficient to justify its creation.

Not only has the discussion about the creation of the market been accompanied by exaggerated claims on both sides, but also a remarkable number of misconceptions have been propagated. I do not have time here to discuss all of the extraordinary arguments that have been put forward, but I think that there are three which have come up with such frequency that they must at least be looked at.

(a) *'A traded options market is just a casino'*
This statement implies a complete misunderstanding of the nature of risk which is, as I pointed out earlier, central to the whole idea. A casino, or for that matter a race track, is in economic terms a machine for creating risk in order that people may gamble on the risk which has been so invented. By contrast any market exists to provide machinery for absorption of *inherent* risk, that is the risk which arises naturally and unavoidably from any in-

3

dustrial or commercial activity. From the economic point of view, if there were no machines for inventing risk, such as casinos, the overall effect would be virtually nil. On the other hand, if there were no machinery for absorbing risk, virtually all economic activity would come to an end.

The creation of a market in traded options does not increase in the slightest the total amount of risk in existence, because for every investor who increases his risk exposure there has necessarily been another investor who has reduced his. The 'risk supply' has therefore not been inflated and all that has happened is that the capacity of the system as a whole to absorb risk has been increased. Nothing could be further from a casino than this.

(b) *'In Chicago only 4% of options are exercised, and therefore 96% of buyers lose money'*

If this deduction were true then it might not in fact be so terrible. On the simplistic assumption which most people make about the identity of the buyers and the sellers in the traded options market (assumptions which, as I have pointed out earlier, are far from necessarily true) then the overall effect of 96% of the buyers losing money would be to transfer resources from gamblers to pensioners, and this would surely be, at least in part, defensible.

In fact, however, the deduction is false and arises from a misunderstanding of how the market actually functions. Because of the existence of a cheap and efficient method for trading in options it is almost invariably true that it is better for somebody who has bought an option to sell that option back into the market (whether at a profit or at a loss) rather than to exercise it. Similarly, a seller will usually prefer to extinguish his liability by purchasing an option to close his position rather than to incur the cost of having the option exercised against him. It could therefore be seen that the high rate of extinction of traded option positions (by transactions in the opposite direction) and the low rate of exercise says a great deal about the cheapness and efficiency of the market, but nothing about the relative profitability of buying and selling.

(c) *'About half of all sellers of traded options are naked, and this is obviously immoral'*

The description of a seller who chooses to cover his liability with cash rather than a specific security as a 'naked writer' is engagingly picturesque, but seems to have produced some fundamental misapprehensions. To assume that it is in some way immoral or even unusual to be prepared to settle a liability with money rather than an identical object is to reduce economic analysis to the level of a barter economy. The insurance company who insures motor cars or super-tankers does not keep a stock of cars or super-tankers in order to be able to replace one which is destroyed in an accident, and there is no more reason why the seller of a traded option should necessarily feel obliged to maintain identical shares to cover his liability. The important thing in the traded options market, as in the insurance market, is to make sure that the participants really have set aside enough money to make ample provision for the liabilities which have been assumed, and money is neither better nor worse than stock to perform this function.

To sum up, I believe strongly that a market in traded options can be useful, both for investors and for the economy as a whole. Investors have the opportunity, if they wish, to modify the risk characteristics of their portfolio so that they correspond more closely to their requirements and to their judgement of future developments. On the other hand, the capacity of the market as a whole to absorb risk is increased, and this can only have beneficial effects on the level of industrial and commercial activity.

TRADED VERSUS TRADITIONAL OPTIONS

In order to appreciate fully the innovatory changes in option trading which were introduced by the CBOE in the early 1970s it is necessary to take a closer look at the structural flaws prevalent in the constitution of the traditional option. Inflexibility is the common theme of most of the criticisms.

(1) Restricted time scale of only three months.
(2) Limited gearing. The buyer of a call option (a 'giver' in the terminology of the traditional option) would be asked to pay a premium to reserve the right to purchase the underlying shares at any time up to expiry of the option three months hence at an agreed price (i.e. the exercise or strike price). This strike price is invariably the offer price of the shares at that time in the Stock Exchange. The premium paid as a percentage of the price of the share will vary depending upon the 'grade' and volatility of the underlying security. The three-month call rate on leading shares may average around 7–8% and, while this provides an obvious measure of gearing, it lacks in degree imaginative variety which could be achieved only by standardisation of the exercise price and expiry date. If the underlying share price at expiry remained exactly where it was three months earlier when the call option was purchased, the option could not be exercised profitably and would have to be abandoned for the loss of the premium plus expenses. If the underlying share price had not moved within a week or a month after the option had been purchased, it could not be exercised and sold without incurring a loss despite the fact that the giver had changed his view totally.

5

(3) The 'taker' of option money in the traditional option market (i.e. the writer of a traded option) found himself in a restricted, inflexible environment. Firstly, he had to wait for a buyer of the option to appear before he could be offered any call money from the option jobber who matched buyer and seller for a fee. Assuming that a buyer materialised and the taker was fortunate enough to be offered the call money, once he had taken it he had to wait until the corresponding buyer made a move (either to exercise or subsequently to abandon the option) before he (the taker) could react. He was able, of course, to job in the under- lying shares against the 'cover' of his option position, but this was both cumbersome and expensive and really defeated the *modus operandi* of option trading. Thus, the level of the premiums offered to the 'taker', irregular in their availability, have been largely insufficiently attractive, particularly in highly volatile markets, to counter the lack of flexibility inherent in a concept that 'locks in' the seller and reduces him largely to passive inaction for the outstanding term of the option. The structure of the traditional option market binds together the buyer and the seller directly even though they are unlikely ever to meet.

The basic innovatory principles governing the CBOE which were to revolutionise option trading were:

(a) standardisation of the exercise price and the expiry date of the option contract, and
(b) fungibility or interchangeability of option contracts which severed the link binding the buyer and seller in the traditional put and call market restoring total flexibility to both parties to the transaction.

In achieving these important changes the CBOE created a primary and an active secondary market in options, enabling the investor both to buy and exercise an option and to buy and sell existing options as well. The importance of standardising the option terms and fungibility as characteristics of listed options necessary for the development of the secondary market cannot be overemphasised. The latter enables each listed option with a common expiry date and strike price to be inter- changeable with any similar listed option. This was achieved in London by the introduction of the London Option Clearing House Limited (LOCH) under the jurisdiction of the Stock Exchange Council. The buyer and the writer of a traded option bargain have a contract only with LOCH which is the issuing house of listed options in London. The buyer relies directly on the clearing house to make good the contract, while the writer's obligation is also to the clearing house and not another broker. Either party to the transaction can terminate his commitment by effecting the appropriate sale or purchase, i.e. reversing the orginal transaction. Another feature of the innovations pioneered by the CBOE is *certificateless trading*.

No certificates of ownership are issued to holders of traded option contracts. In London, LOCH maintains a daily record of contracts held and written, and every member firm of the Stock Exchange is required to keep a continuous record of the option contracts held or written by its clients. Ownership or the writing of option contracts is evidenced by contract notes and statements issued by brokers to their clients. A broker's contract note will look something like the one in Figure 1.1 and should contain the type of information shown.

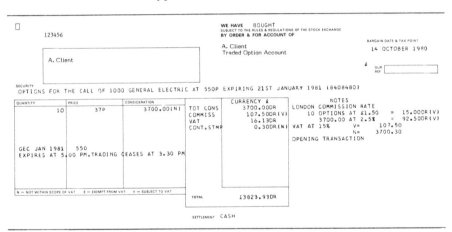

Figure 1.1. Sample contract note showing the purchase of ten GEC Jan. 550 at 37p (to open). Total cost £3,823.93 ($10 \times 1,000 \times 37 = $ £3,700 plus expenses as detailed above) for expiry on 21 January 1981. Settlement is for cash, i.e. the following business day (15.10.80). When the position is sold the contract note will record that it is a closing transaction. Each account is allocated a number (shown as no. 123456 in the top left-hand corner) recognised by LOCH for clearing purposes.

It follows that, since the option contracts held or written by clients and the day-to-day margin arrangements are in the books of the brokers through whom the original transactions were made, it is important that closing transactions should be made through the broker who executed the opening purchase or sale. A client may transfer option positions open in his name from one broker to another only by making a written request to his former broker to transfer his account to another broker who has agreed to accept it. The concept of certificate-less trading is an eminently practical and sensible administrative step forward: by reducing considerably the physical volume of paper (giving title of ownership) in existence, it both speeds up the process of settlement and, in the medium term, renders it cheaper to effect. It has been an unqualified success in America where the volume of contracts traded has grown astronomically. The concept of certificateless trading, however, is founded on the basic premise that the holder of a traded option contract must be able to assume total confidence in the ability of the clearing house to ensure, at any time, the fulfilment of the terms of the contract which he or she has bought. The system of guarantees supporting London traded options has four component parts, designed in total to create or substantiate the confidence both required and expected by potential investors.

(1) Every traded option contract is secured by the deposit with LOCH of the appropriate cover or margin. In the event of a writer's default this cover or margin could be used by LOCH to implement the terms of the contract, any excess being returned to the writer.

(2) If margin deposited with LOCH should prove inadequate to fulfil the contracts to which it relates, the entire resources of the member firm which had acted as broker to the defaulting writer, together with the entire resources of its clearing agent, will be available.

(3) Standing behind the resources of each clearing member firm will be the total sum of the guarantees of £125,000 given by each of the other clearing members.

(4) Finally, should these substantial resources be exhausted, investors would be able to make a claim on the Stock Exchange Compensation Fund.

It is to be assumed that 'guarantees' of this substance and magnitude will satisfy even the most hostile, hard-line traditionalist who feels vulnerable and somewhat uncomfortable without physical possession of the more customary documentary evidence of good title.

Most of the innovations that were introduced by the CBOE in America were simple in concept and straightforward in implementation. These changes, coupled with a planned educational programme started two years before the market opened and backed up and substantiated by first class literature and heavy use of media advertising, left the American public well schooled and eager to start. As an exercise in intelligent forward planning and intensive marketing it cannot be faulted and has reaped the rewards it justly deserved. The quite astounding success that the CBOE achieved right from the outset (1973) was even more remarkable bearing in mind that the American stock market (in line with most of the remaining major stock markets of the world) was about to witness one of the steepest and most pro-longed falls on record.

Opening on 26 April 1973, the average daily volume for May (in contracts) was 1,600 and the total for the month 34,500. By October the figure had swelled to 115,000 daily and 266,000 over the month. One year later (October 1974) these two figures had expanded to 39,000 and 899,000 respectively. The month of March 1975 witnessed over one million contracts traded, and ten months later (January 1976) recorded a total of 2.6 million contracts with an average daily volume of 123,000 traded. A quite staggering growth rate! The Amex and Philadelphia option exchanges opened in 1975, followed by the Pacific exchange in 1976. Put options were introduced by the CBOE in 1977. At the time of writing, the Amex exchange lists call options on 77 stocks, Philadelphia on 51, Pacific on 35 and the CBOE on 120. Over the four exchanges 131 puts are traded.

On 13 November 1980 new records were set as Amex traded 226,100 contracts, Philadelphia 60,026 and the Pacific Exchange 48,752, all sur-passing previous highs. Only the CBOE at 401,222 was shy of its best day on record (17 April 1978) when 402,440 calls were traded, helping to create a total for the month of over 3.3 million contracts. What a marvellous success story it has been! Against such a background it is difficult sometimes to appreciate just why it has been so arduous to get the European Option Exchange and the London Traded Options Market off the ground even within the stockbroking fraternity. Never-theless, tortoise-like (in comparison with the American hares) we may be in Europe, but we will get there in the end, almost despite ourselves. The volume figures transposed on to Figure 1.2 show the development of volume in the London Traded Options Market to date. We have a long way to go!

For the majority of investors in Europe traded options should be considered and utilised as a new, key tool in the achievement of invest-ment objectives: their unique advantages are numerous and they offer

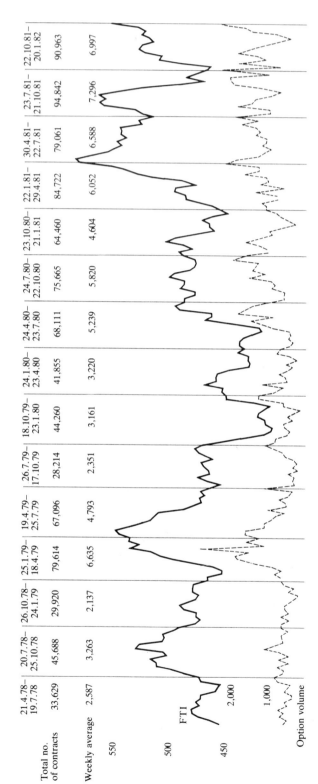

Total no. of contracts	21.4.78–19.7.78	20.7.78–25.10.78	26.10.78–24.1.79	25.1.79–18.4.79	19.4.79–25.7.79	26.7.79–17.10.79	18.10.79–23.1.80	24.1.80–23.4.80	24.4.80–23.7.80	24.7.80–22.10.80	23.10.80–21.1.81	22.1.81–29.4.81	30.4.81–22.7.81	23.7.81–21.10.81	22.10.81–20.1.82
	33,629	45,688	29,920	79,614	67,096	28,214	44,260	41,855	68,111	75,665	64,460	84,722	79,061	94,842	90,963
Weekly average	2,587	3,263	2,137	6,635	4,793	2,351	3,161	3,220	5,239	5,820	4,604	6,052	6,588	7,296	6,997

Figure 1.2. FTI 30 shares/option volume, March 1978–January 1982.

almost total flexibility. A well-prepared option scheme can be tailored to meet the requirements of most investors at most times. Later in the book I will endeavour to highlight various investment strategies that may be employed through the medium of traded options in order to capitalise on market movements of varying magnitude. Before I can do that it is necessary to consider some of the basic investment characteristics of an option contract and define a few of the terms employed.

2

Basic terms and definitions

An **option** is a negotiable contract involving a buyer and seller. The buyer is willing to purchase or sell a specific number of shares at a fixed price within an agreed time period, for a price, i.e. the **option premium**; the seller is willing to grant these rights also for a price. A **call option** grants the purchaser the right to buy shares from the writer (i.e. seller). A **put option** grants the purchaser the right to sell shares to the writer. The essential components of such an option are:

(1) a description of the item that the option buyer may purchase from the writer of the option;
(2) the price at which the item may be purchased;
(3) the time period during which the buyer of the option must exercise or lose his right to purchase. If the option buyer chooses not to exercise his purchase rights during the time allowed – usually because he deems it not to his advantage to do so – the option simply expires. It ceases to exist.

Class
All options on the shares of a particular company constitute a **class** of traded options (whether **puts** or **calls**). If the London market lists call options on the underlying securities of 18 companies, there will be 18 classes in existence.

Option premium
The **option premium** is the price paid by the buyer and received by the seller for the rights granted by the option. This sum of money is kept by the seller whether the option is exercised or not, and is expressed as an amount per option on a single share of the underlying security. The

premium is the *only* variable term of the contract between purchaser and seller, and will reflect the normal function of supply and demand for the underlying security, its volatility and the outstanding time value of the option itself.

Exercise price

The price at which the option buyer may purchase the underlying security from the writer is known as the **exercise** or **strike price**. When a new class of traded options is introduced to the market, two exercise prices are established for the class, one below and one above the current price of the shares. The one below the current price of the shares is termed **in-the-money** and the one above the current price of the shares is referred to as **out-of-the-money**. If the underlying share price moves dramatically up or down, additional strike prices may be introduced (the normal interval between strike prices is approximately 10% of the underlying share price). If the underlying share price swings around substantially, it is perfectly possible to have several in-the-money and several out-of-the-money options being traded at the same time. If the price of the underlying security is the same as a particular strike price, the option is termed **at-the-money**.

Expiry dates

The maximum life of a traded option is nine months and the expiry dates are arranged on a quarterly cycle so that, at any one time, there are always three different expiry dates listed for each class (i.e. an option life of three, six and nine months). Two different cycles are employed: the first is January, April, July and October and the second February, May, August and November. At the time of writing ten option classes are on the January–October cycle and seven are on the February–November cycle. When a new class is introduced, the Stock Exchange allocates it permanently to one of these cycles. As the January options expire, the options already trading to April and July will be joined by an October expiry so there will be options for April, July and October, having respectively three, six and nine months' life ahead of them. Traded options generally expire on the third or fourth Wednesday of the final month of their life, although occasionally the incidence of Bank Holidays can distort the pattern. The idea is that the options will always expire on the last day but two of a Stock Exchange fortnightly settlement period. In practice, these dates are fixed well in advance by the Stock Exchange and are always shown on a contract note issued by a broker (see Figure 1.1).

Series

All options in a class which share the same exercise price and expiry date constitute a **series**. If Imperial Group Limited (IMP) were priced at 65p in the market, there would be six series available, as follows:

IMP Feb. 60	IMP May 60	IMP Aug. 60
IMP Feb. 70	IMP May 70	IMP Aug. 70

A new traded option series will be introduced only where:

(1) the price of the underlying stock:
  (a) exceeds the highest exercise price in the class at the close of the Traded Options Market on four successive business days;

  or

  (b) on any business day rises to a level midway between the highest current exercise price in the class and the exercise price of the next series to be introduced.

(2) the price of the underlying stock:
  (a) falls below the lowest exercise price in the class at the close of the Traded Options Market on four successive business days;

  or

  (b) on any business day falls to a level midway between the lowest current exercise price in the class and the exercise price of the next series to be introduced.

Unit of trading

The minimum unit of trading is one contract which (in London) normally represents the options on 1,000 shares of the underlying security. This figure may, however, be altered in particular circumstances due to share capitalisations or other factors. For example, the unit of trading for Vaal Reef is in respect of 100 ordinary shares of Rand 0.5 nominal. Vaal Reef traded options are quoted in US dollars and fractions of dollars.

All orders in traded options should refer to the number of contracts in which an investor wishes to deal and not to the number of shares of the underlying security to which the option contract relates. Hence, if an investor wishes to trade in the options on 10,000 shares of the underlying security, he would place an order for 10 contracts and not 10,000 options. A contract is indivisible and orders cannot be executed in fractions of a contract.

Time of payment
The rules of the London Stock Exchange require that all bargains in traded options are transacted for settlement before 10.00 a.m. on the following business day. Stockbrokers are obliged to require their clients to provide them with the stipulated premium (if a purchaser) or the requisite margin or cover (if a writer) before that time.

Option price service and volume guide
Between the hours of 9.35 a.m. and 3.30 p.m. each business day, investors will be able to request both up-to-date option prices (including the price at which the last deal in a particular series was effected) and the volume figures from one of the stockbrokers specialising in traded options. The following day the *Financial Times* and the *Daily Telegraph* publish the closing option data which will include a breakdown of the volume transacted in *each* option series traded as well as the cumulative total. The closing price of the option series quoted at 3.30 p.m. each day will be the **offer price**. The *Daily Telegraph* publishes each day almost the entire option list, irrespective of whether or not a particular series has traded at all during the day (see Figure 2.1). The *Financial Times*, on the other hand, has a tendency to publish the closing prices only of the series in which some volume was transacted.

Additionally, a broker will be able to provide up-to-date information regarding the **open-interest position**, i.e. the number of listed option contracts outstanding (open) at any particular time. Open-interest figures are available on each option series.

UNDERLYING SECURITIES

European Option Exchange: Amsterdam

Option market symbol

American stocks (units of 100 shares per contract)
Expiry cycle: Nov., Feb., May, (Aug.)

Boeing	(C & P)*	BOEI
Occidental Petroleum	(C)	OCCI
Schlumberger	(C)	SLUM

Expiry cycle: Dec., Mar., Jun., (Sept.)

General Motors	(C)	GM
Sears	(C)	S

*(Calls & puts)

LONDON TRADED OPTIONS

Underlying securities · Expiry cycle

Option	Ex'cise Price	January Cl. Off	Vol.	April Cl. Off	Vol.	July Cl. Off	Vol.
	p	p		p		p	
BP	330	162	—	170	—	—	—
BP	360	134	—	142	—	—	—
BP	390	106	—	118	—	—	—
BP	420	82	4	94	20	110	—
BP	460	54	108	70	10	86	40
BP	500	32	106	48	—	66	20
Comm. Union	120	45	—	—	—	—	—
Comm. Union	130	35	—	—	—	—	—
Comm. Union	140	25	25	31	50	37	—
Comm. Union	160	12	2	17	10	22	—
Comm. Union	180	3	145	9	43	14	—
Cons. Gold	460	155	—	—	—	—	—
Cons. Gold	500	118	55	140	—	—	—
Cons. Gold	550	77	2	105	—	—	—
Cons. Gold	600	45	3	80	—	97	—
Cons. Gold	650	27	75	55	11	72	10
Cons. Gold	700	16	20	33	5	52	—
Courtaulds	50	20	10	21½	—	—	—
Courtaulds	60	12	—	15	—	17	—
Courtaulds	70	5½	3	9½	14	12	6
Courtaulds	80	3	5	—	—	—	—
GEC	330	265	—	—	—	—	—
GEC	360	235	—	—	—	—	—
GEC	390	205	—	—	—	—	—
GEC	420	175	—	—	—	—	—
GEC	460	140	—	165	—	—	—
GEC	500	100	21	132	—	155	—
GEC	550	63	37	100	1	122	—
GEC	600	37	32	72	1	95	—
Grand Met.	120	39	—	—	—	—	—
Grand Met.	130	30	—	—	—	—	—
Grand Met.	140	23	65	28	—	33	—
Grand Met.	160	10	22	18	16	23	1
Grand Met.	180	3½	16	10	—	15	—
ICI	300	55	—	64	—	74	—
ICI	330	34	1	44	2	54	—
ICI	360	16	10	28	—	38	—
ICI	390	7	1	16	—	—	—
Land Securities	323	77	—	—	—	—	—
Land Securities	353	47	23	—	—	—	—
Land Securities	360	—	—	62	—	75	—
Land Securities	390	25	76	42	—	55	—
Land Securities	420	9	8	25	10	38	5
Marks & Spencer	80	36	—	—	—	—	—
Marks & Spencer	90	26	—	31	—	—	—
Marks & Spencer	100	17	8	23	—	27	—
Marks & Spencer	110	9½	15	16	—	19	—
Marks & Spencer	120	4½	2	11	—	15	—
Shell	390	100	—	—	—	—	—
Shell	420	72	—	86	—	100	—
Shell	460	44	1	58	—	74	—
Shell	500	27	22	40	—	56	—

Expiry cycle

Option	Price	NOVEMBER Cl. Off	Vol.	FEBRUARY Cl. Off	Vol.	MAY Cl. Off	Vol.
Imperial Grp.	70	6	19	12	7	14	3
Imperial Grp.	80	1	6	5	17	8	12
Imperial Grp.	90	2	—	4½	—	—	—
Lonrho	94	12	—	22	1	—	—
Lonrho	100	—	—	—	—	22	—
Lonrho	104	3	59	14	—	—	—
Lonrho	110	—	—	—	—	14	3
Lonrho	114	¾	210	7½	—	—	—
Lonrho	120	¼	—	6	8	10	3
P & O	100	25	—	27½	—	—	—
P & O	110	15	—	18½	—	27	—
P & O	120	5	20	13½	—	20	—
P & O	130	2½	4	8½	4	12½	—
P & O	140	1½	—	5½	—	9	—
Racal	260	93	60	—	—	—	—
Racal	280	73	1	89	—	105	—
Racal	300	53	5	72	—	88	—
Racal	330	23	89	50	39	68	—
Racal	360	7	—	34	13	52	—
R.T.Z.	384	68	1	87	—	—	—
R.T.Z.	414	38	—	63	—	83	—
R.T.Z.	454	8	37	38	1	56	—
R.T.Z.	494	2	—	20	—	38	—

Closing premium (offer price)

Figure 2.1. Table of London traded option information as published in the *Daily Telegraph*, 12 November 1980. (Reproduced with permission of the *Daily Telegraph*.)

16

Option market symbol
American stocks (units of 100 shares per contract) – *cont.*
Expiry cycle: Jan., Apr., Jul., (Oct.)

American Telegram & Telephone	(C)	ATT
Citicorp	(C)	CITI
Eastman Kodak	(C)	KODA
Exxon	(C)	EXON
IBM	(C & P)	IBM
Polaroid	(C)	POLA
Xerox	(C)	XERO

Belgian stocks (units of 100 shares per contract)
Expiry cycle: Jan., Apr., Jul., (Oct.)

Petrofina	(C & P)	PETR

Dutch stocks (units of 100 shares per contract)
Expiry cycle: Jan., Apr., Jul., (Oct.)

AKZO	(C & P)	AKZO
Algemene Bank Nederland	(C)	ABN
Amsterdam Rotterdam Bank	(C)	AMRO
Heinekens Bierbrouwerij	(C & P)	HEIN
Hoogovens	(C)	HOOG
KLM	(C & P)	KLM
National Nederlanden	(C & P)	NATN
Philips Lamp	(C & P)	PHIL
Royal Dutch	(C & P)	OLIE
Unilever	(C & P)	UNIL

French stocks (units of 100 shares per contract)
Expiry cycle: Jan., Apr., Jul., (Oct.)

Peugeot Citroën	(C)	PSA
Source Perrier	(C)	PU
CSF Thompson	(C)	CSF

German stocks (units of 50 shares per contract)
Expiry cycle: Nov., Feb., May, (Aug.)

BASF	(C)	BAS
Mannesman	(C)	MMW
Siemens	(C)	SIE
Veba	(C)	VEB
Volkswagen	(C)	VW

Traded Options Market: London

Option market symbol

Expiry cycle: Jan., Apr., Jul., Oct.

British Petroleum Company	(C & P)	BP
Commercial Union Assurance Company	(C)	CUA
Consolidated Goldfields	(C & P)	CGF
Courtaulds	(C)	CTD
General Electric Company	(C & P)	GEC
Grand Metropolitan	(C & P)	GMH
Imperial Chemical Industries	(C & P)	ICI
Land Securities Investment Trust	(C)	LSI
Marks & Spencer	(C)	M & S
'Shell' Transport & Trading Company	(C & P)	SHL

Expiry cycle: Feb., May, Aug., Nov.

Barclays Bank	(C & P)	BBL
Imperial Group	(C & P)	IMP
London & Scottish Marine Oil Company	(C)	LMO
Lonrho	(C & P)	LNR
Peninsular and Oriental Steam Navigation Company	(C)	P & O
Racal Electronics	(C & P)	RCL
Rio Tinto Zinc Corporation	(C & P)	RTZ
Vaal Reef Exploration	(C & P)	VRF

SELECTION OF UNDERLYING STOCKS

If traded options are to fulfil their proper role within the securities industry, the market must have both depth and liquidity. Depth is the term used to denote the size of bargain which may readily be transacted; liquidity refers to the total amount of turnover in the market. They are not synonymous terms. For example, it is possible to imagine a market in which, from time to time, very large numbers of options changed hands, but where on some days it became difficult to deal in even a few contracts. On the other hand, a market might exist in which it was always easy to deal in small amounts, but where large orders created severe problems.

An ideal market in traded options should have a consistently good volume of trade and should be able to handle large orders without their exercising a disproportionate influence on the level of prices. The selection of underlying stocks for option trading is critical in this respect. The option market will not have depth and liquidity unless those characteristics are present in the share market, and so the qualifications for selection must be stringent. The following criteria will be observed.

(1) The company's shares must be listed on the Stock Exchange.
(2) During the five years prior to the introduction of option trading, the company must not have defaulted on the payment of any interest, dividend or sinking fund instalment, or committed any breach of the provisions of any borrowing limitation, of any loan stock or of the Articles of Association which, in the opinion of the Stock Exchange, would render the company unsuitable for option trading.
(3) The company must have a substantial equity market capitalisation and there must have been a free and active market in the shares for at least two years previously.
(4) The company must have at least 10,000 equity shareholders.

Position limits

Even the most ardent fan of the traded options market must agree that it would be manifestly wrong that option trading should, at any time, be allowed to dominate trading in the underlying security. For this reason, limits are essential on both the total number of options which may be in existence at any one time and the number of options which any single group of investors may hold. Strict controls are thus imposed.

Limits on the total of options in issue

The following limits are placed upon the number of options which may be outstanding at any one time.

(1) The total number of shares represented by options in any class registered by LOCH is not allowed to exceed 10% of the quoted, issued equity share capital of the company.
(2) The total number of shares represented by options in any class registered by LOCH and not covered by the deposit of the underlying security (i.e. written by uncovered writers) is not allowed to exceed 5% of the quoted, issued equity share capital of the company.

Limits of position of holders and writers

The number of options which may be held or written on behalf of anyone, or several parties acting in concert, is limited to 1,000 contracts of any one series and to 2,000 contracts of any one class in total. For the purpose of this rule, contracts held and contracts written will be considered separately and will not be aggregated.

3

Purchasing traded call options

Most call options are bought on the assumption that the underlying share and the option to purchase it at a fixed price (the strike or exercise price) will increase in value at some point prior to expiry. If this duly materialises, the option can then be sold to another investor who believes that the option will increase further in value or will be profitable to exercise into the underlying security. Although American experience in particular over the past eight years clearly reveals that the vast majority of call option purchases are subsequently sold (as closing option sales), nevertheless the use of options to forward buy the underlying security is a valid and often extremely profitable strategy (in terms of return on capital employed) in modern investment theory.

As we have seen earlier, a call option is simply a contract involving a buyer and a seller, the buyer willing to purchase certain option rights and the seller willing to grant these same option rights for a price. That price is the option premium.

FACTORS AFFECTING OPTION PRICES

What then are the main factors and influences which determine the amount of the premium for a particular option at a particular time, and what causes the premium to increase or decrease?

Normal supply/demand criteria for option prices will be dependent upon rising or falling underlying share prices in general. During times of rising stock market prices there is an increased interest in purchasing options that convey the right to buy certain shares at an agreed, fixed price. Potential sellers of options will be reluctant to commit themselves and thus option premium levels will rise. The converse is true during periods of declining stock market prices where there is greater interest in writing call options than in purchasing them: the net result is that premiums will decline. Additionally, the main factors that interact to influence the level of call option premiums can be summarised as follows.

(1) The relationship between the prevailing market price of the underlying shares and the exercise price of the option is import-ant. 'In-the-money' calls (where the exercise price is below the market price) will command higher (though not necessarily more expensive) premiums than either 'at-the-money' calls (where the exercise price is the same as the market price of the stock) or 'out-of-the-money' calls (where the exercise price is above the market price of the stock). The reason for this price differential among the three 'categories' is, I trust, straightforward and easily understood: the 'in-the-money' option, by definition, commands a measure of intrinsic value. This is illustrated by Table 3.1 of RTZ option prices (expiry date 27 August 1980).

Table 3.1

On 20 June 1980 the ordinary share price of RTZ was 423p.

RTZ *stock price (p)*	*August option* *exercise prices (p)*	*August option* *prices (p)*	*Intrinsic* *value (p)*
423	300	132	123
423	330	103	93
423	360	75	63
423	390	50	33
423	420	35	3
423	460	13	No intrinsic value

While the share price stood at 423, all the August options with exercise prices running from 300 to 420 had intrinsic (tangible) values of varying magnitude.

(2) Premiums will be affected by the outstanding *time value* of the option: the more time remaining until the expiry date, the higher the premium will be. Time value is thus the premium over the

intrinsic value (if any) of the option. As the expiry date of the option approaches, the time value portion of the option price progressively sinks to zero. Thus, purchasers of call options are buying time: a November option for a particular share will normally command a higher premium than an otherwise identical August option because the time scale is longer over which the underlying shares can rise in price. To illustrate the point the earlier example of RTZ has been used in Table 3.2 to compare premium levels and time values between the August and November option expiry.

Table 3.2

RTZ strike prices (p)	*August option prices (p)*	*Time value*	*November option prices (p)*	*Time value*
330	103	10	115	22
360	75	12	90	27
390	50	17	67	34
420	35	32	47	44
460	13	13	28	28

(3) Premiums will tend not to increase or decrease point for point with the price movement of the underlying share prices *unless and until* the option reaches parity (i.e. the exercise price plus the premium equates to the prevailing market price).

(4) Premium levels will be affected quite dramatically by the *volatility* of the underlying shares: widely fluctuating shares will command higher option premiums than those traditionally trading within a narrow price range. The concept of volatility requires further study and explanation, and it is considered in more detail below.

Volatility

The importance of volatility (i.e. the propensity of a stock to respond to a market move) to purchasers of call options cannot be stressed too strongly. As time is the ally of the writer of options, volatility is the running-mate of the buyer of options. It may sound obvious but it still needs to be spelt out so that no one is under any illusion: option price movement is almost entirely dependent upon the movement of the underlying share price. I have said 'almost entirely', the exception to this rule being the somewhat rare occurrence when an option price is adjusted upwards (i.e. a change in its valuation) without a corresponding move in the underlying share. While such a phenomenon can sometimes herald a dramatic and highly profitable change in the rating of the underlying security, it can also reflect nothing more than the over-enthusiasm and greed of the herd, which can have disastrous results for option purchasers. The following example helps to illustrate the need for judgement and circumspection in such an instance.

In the four bull market moves in the FT Index which took place between July 1978 and November 1980, the price performance of Courtaulds was appalling. Indeed, it was notable only for the magnitude of its under-performance of the average over this time scale. Hence, the shares had achieved a low volatility (beta) rating and were not to be recommended as an attractive option purchase for those wishing to capitalise on any upward move in the market as a whole.

Nevertheless, with everything apparently going against it, the Courtaulds share price displayed remarkable perversion, rising over 35% in the five weeks between the end of May and early July 1980. An October in-the-money option at the end of May would have cost a little over 6% of the share price in time value; by early July, despite the loss of over one month's duration, the in-the-money October option would have cost over 10% of the share price in time value. Was this 'changed' valuation of the options signalling a new stock market star in its ascendency, or was the herd simply getting carried away? A cautionary statement from the chairman in his mid-July AGM report ended the speculation as the shares dropped 17% in two trading days, thus wiping out much of the progress that had been achieved over the preceding month. The in-the-money October options were decimated!

Historically, certain stocks have always tended to respond more positively than others to a general market move. In any index some shares will consistently and clearly out-perform others. The stock with the history of the greatest positive price response within the framework of a market move will command the highest beta. This rating will reflect the interaction of numerous factors. These include historic earnings growth (whether largely organic or acquisitional) and the dividend payout record – a reflection of management dynamism or otherwise; specific areas of activity – for example, in recent years growth prospects in electronics would tend to be more highly rated than in textiles or heavy engineering; the degree of dependence upon particular markets or geographical territories; the capital or labour intensity of the business, etc. While a high beta does not guarantee that the stock will necessarily rise in price, it does, however, offer reasonable security that, if a decision on market timing is correct either of the stock in isolation or of the market as a whole, then the high beta stock will respond positively. That is precisely what the option buyer is seeking; that is his *only* justification for paying a premium (and often a substantial premium) – for the privilege of buying time. Option valuation levels can and do vary dramatically between different companies, and the volatility rating of the underlying security is a major determinant of such a differential.

A glance at the option valuation levels of the marginally in-the-money series (with an expiry date of 22 October) relating to BP, Consolidated Goldfields and Courtaulds at the end of May 1980, prior to the sharp 25% rally in the FT Index, will highlight the valuation differential (see Table 3.3).

Table 3.3

Company	Stock price (p)	In-the-money option	Option price (p)	Time value	Time value as % of share price
BP	331	Oct. 330	40	39 (40−1)	11.8
CGF	470	Oct. 460	60	50 (60−10)	10.6
CTD	72	Oct. 70	6.5	4.5 (6.5−2)	6.3

BP and CGF were considered high volatility stocks and their option premiums reflected this factor. CTD, as we discussed earlier, had a low volatility rating and thus its October in-the-money option was considerably cheaper than the other two, as the final column of the table shows. Additionally, both BP and CGF were due to go ex dividend within the October expiry time scale, making their options even more expensive. (I deal with the important subject of dividends in detail later, but the effect of a stock price being adjusted ex the net dividend within the option period obviously goes against the option buyer who does not intend exercising into the underlying security-cum-dividend.) The net dividend adjustment is often not insubstantial to the price of the option – in BP's case in the instance above the shares were due to go ex 5½p net on 10 September.

Since volatility is such an important concept in a market of traded options, I have analysed four 'bull' moves in the FT Index between

July 1978 and November 1980. These moves may be summarised as follows.

(1) 1978 July to September   + 18%
(2) 1979 February to May   + 25%
(3) 1980 January to February   + 18%
(4) 1980 June to November   + 25%

Over these four cycles the closing-day low and subsequent high price achieved has been recorded as a percentage gain for each of the underlying securities upon which options were then listed, and placed in order of magnitude (see Table 3.4).

Table 3.4

1978 *July/September*		1979 *February/May*		1979/1980 *November/January*		1980 *June/Nov.*	
RCL	44%	RTZ	60%	CGF	112%	GEC	77%
GEC	30%	GMH	54%	RTZ	80%	RCL	60%
M & S*	28%	M & S	53%	LNR	62%	LNR	53%
LSI	21%	CGF	47%	RCL	37%	BP	51%
RTZ	20%	RCL	46%	M & S	33%	M & S	46%
GMH	20%	SHL	45%	SHL	27%	SHL	37%
FTI	**18%**	GEC	45%	LSI	27%	GMH	28%
IMP	17%	P & O	44%	ICI	26%	RTZ	26%
ICI	16%	LNR	43%	BP	25%	**FTI**	**25%**
LNR	14%	BP	39%	CUA	24%	LSI	21%
P & O	14%	CUA	32%	GEC	24%	CGF	18%
BP	10%	IMP	30%	P & O	20%	CUA	16%
CUA	10%	LSI	27%	GMH	19%	P & O	15%
SHL	9%	**FTI**	**25%**	**FTI**	**18%**	IMP	4%
CGF	7.5%	ICI	20%	IMP	17%	ICI	–
CTD	6%	CTD	6%	CTD	11%	CTD	–

*Adjusted for 100% scrip issue: August 1978.

Over these trading periods only GEC, Racal, M & S, Rio Tinto Zinc and Grand Metropolitan have consistently bettered the performance of the FT Index. An analysis of the annual relative price performance of these stocks taken back to 1974 reveals the same results. In my opinion the probability is that they will contine to out-perform the average. Lonrho, BP and Shell have 'picked up' in the performance league since 1979, Land Securities have been there or thereabouts throughout the period, while Consolidated Goldfields, P & O and Commercial Union have been 'patchy' in the extreme. Imperial Tobacco, Imperial Chemical Industries and the luckless Courtaulds have 'brought up the rear' with alarming consistency.

In circumstances which change as rapidly as they tend to in the modern investment world, beta analysis must remain a relatively inexact science. While the need for flexibility in the interpretation of likely price movement remains of paramount importance, nevertheless the historical price performance of a share, in my opinion, has a great deal of validity in predicting its *future* action. Let me stress, once again, that I am not saying that past history can foretell whether a stock is likely to go up or down, or that it can measure the extent of a move against the market. However, certain stocks have displayed a historic consistency for moving up (or down) sharply as the market as a whole has moved up (or down). The probability remains that these stocks will do so again and again.

Thus, if it is possible to designate general rules or guidelines regarding the beta factor and its role in the choice of which stocks/options to select, they might read as follows.

(1) If a general market rise is anticipated, select the high beta stocks and their ancillary options. The premiums (i.e. time value) relating to these options will undoubtedly be more expensive (i.e. higher as a percentage of the share price) than a comparable low beta equivalent. More often than not, in my opinion, the higher price is justified by the greater probability that the higher beta stock will respond with superior speed and magnitude.

(2) By the same token, the low beta stocks/options should be left well alone unless there is a compelling case for buying the individual stock in question. Beware of a sudden change in an option valuation. A low beta stock will have a history of poor relative price performance: this is unlikely to change quickly.

(3) Nevertheless, the change from low to high beta valuation can produce substantial profits for those who correctly anticipate the transition. In an endeavour to capitalise upon such a phenomenon, effect the following.

(a) Study the price volatility of the individual stock relative to general market moves over a five- to ten-year time scale.

(b) For pictorial ease, plot a daily chart of the price movement of the stock on a closing day basis, and attentively watch for patterns of activity that might foreshadow a break out of a well-defined trading range; resistance or resilience levels that develop over a given time scale; patterns of share price movement contrary to the general trend (i.e. relative price performance).

(c) Relate any such movements intelligently to the imminence or otherwise of published figures/dividend dates/company announcements, etc.

(d) Monitor any trend of volume activity in the individual option series, noting the time scale involved.

(e) Review the whole against the degree to which the market is over-bought or over-sold at the time; various statistical measurements of this factor are published regularly in the financial press.

REASONS FOR BUYING CALL OPTIONS

(1) *Limited capital risk*
The cost of the option (premium plus expenses) is the maximum capital loss that may be sustainable: this would be the extent of any financial liability in the transaction irrespective of what happened to the price of the underlying security.

(2) *Dealing forward in anticipation of future cash flows*
Traded options can be used to secure the predetermined price for a future purchase of the underlying security in the light of cash-flow projections. An investor who anticipates a sum of cash from the maturity of a fixed-interest investment, a term deposit, the sale of an asset or a financial gift, for example, may wish to capitalise on a rising stock market in the intervening months. The purchase of a traded option on a three-, six- or nine-month time scale will enable him to establish now the price he will eventually pay for the underlying security.

(3) *Buying options as an insurance policy in portfolio management*
It is possible to design a strategy which involves the purchase of call options covering the same number of shares that would otherwise be acquired in the normal way, and investing the balance of the proceeds in a fixed-income instrument or even leaving it on deposit. Such a strategy, which can be most beneficial in an era of high interest rates, offers the investor some 'insurance' against the contingency of adverse, short-term movements in the underlying stock while, at the same time, offering positive cover should the shares rise sharply. If high interest

rates persist for some considerable time (the United Kingdom experience in 1980 is a good example), it is an enticing prospect for the astute investor to enjoy these rates on the bulk of his capital, leaving possibly up to 20% liquid to be used at particular points in the cycle to gear up the portfolio through option purchases. In my earlier coverage of volatility I analysed four bull moves in the F T Index which took place between July 1978 and November 1980. It is abundantly clear from the statistics that, in modern markets, bull rises are violent and of short duration. If the investor is able to read these moves successfully, he can achieve the best of both worlds: a high return and a geared option portfolio in sensible proportions of capital commitment.

(4) *Buying options for equity gearing*

Most buyers of call options are in pursuit of gearing, the mechanism that enables them to benefit from an increase in the value of the underlying share with a consideration commitment equal to a mere fraction of the cost of purchasing the share itself. The buyer of a call option thus anticipates potentially large profits from a relatively small investment with a built-in predetermined risk. The gearing that can be achieved through traded options can be staggering: during the January 1980 'bull' rally, a 14% upward movement in Land Securities over a three-week time scale produced a tenfold rise in the January 260 series (from 2 to 20).

It might be perfectly permissible for the majority of equity investors, bored and dissatisfied over many decades of relatively unprofitable and unexciting investment performance from leading shares in their portfolios, to assume that an occurrence such as the LSI January 260s was a once-and-for-all phenomenon, something akin to winning the pools. I must tell you that it is not! Quite the opposite: it is unusual not to find at least one startling percentage performance materialising each quarter. It is an enticing prospect! In order to translate the prospect into actuality (and more important, to capitalise upon it) the investor will require skill, discipline, dedication and hard work. But it can be achieved!

STRATEGIES FOR BUYING CALL OPTIONS

Choice of option series

To the uninitiated, the choice of which option to select and over what time scale can sometimes seem a bewildering prospect. It should not be considered so. The array of option series offers immense flexibility and wide freedom of expression to effect the degree of optimism and enthusiasm expressed for either a particular share or an anticipated general market move. The wide selection of option series usually presented is formidable only in the discipline that it demands from the investor in regularising and formalising his investment strategy. Before a sensible choice of option can be made, a decision on or measurement of how bullish he feels for the underlying security and the anticipated time scale of the move must be crystallised. As I have said before, the options cannot move on their own; they can go nowhere without a movement in the underlying security. The extent and timing of such a move is the only relevant problem to be faced up to, but the issue cannot be fudged! It requires an investment discipline uncommon in most investors in the underlying security simply because, at this end, there is no time penalty involved. In dealing in the underlying security the investor is not faced with a declared time scale over which his expectations must be achieved. While the hope endures that the shares perform as quickly as possible, a series of events which delays that process is unfortunate but not critical. In a limited life medium one does not have the luxury of such inexactitude: in option purchases time acts against the buyer as the asset 'wastes' away, each day eroding its value, until expiry, when it ceases to exist.

Timing is thus of paramount importance if the rewards, which may be considerable, are to be reaped. Once the subject of traded options is thoroughly understood and appreciated by the general public it seems unlikely that any private investor considering investing capital in any of the shares listing options will not put a varying proportion of the cash involved directly into one of the options.

Which options to buy and which time scale to select

There can be few meaningful standard 'rules' which will apply to each investment opportunity as it presents itself. However, various option categories offer an outlet for the expression of differing degrees of optimism. It is often suggested that in-the-money options (exercise price below market price) are the most conservative choice, offering the investor the comfort of some intrinsic value. This is true, but it is also often suggested (if only by innuendo) that, because of this factor, the in-the-money option is 'safer' than its brother, the out-of-the-money option (exercise price above the market price), which thus offers greater gearing but no intrinsic value at the time.

29

While this is a perfectly reasonable supposition in a rising market, it can be a dangerous assumption if treated as a general rule. All option purchases theoretically risk total loss of capital committed to them; the in-the-money option ties up larger sums of money and thus risks a greater capital loss. The fact that it offers some intrinsic value at the time of purchase is no guarantee whatsoever that the underlying stock will not fall and thus threaten the larger capital outlay than would have been relevant in a purchase of the out-of-the-money series.

In-the-money versus out-of-the-money

The choice of which option series to select often provides the investor with a major headache. It shouldn't. In the main, the process of selection should follow a well-ordered, disciplined pattern, starting with the most important decision of all: how bullish the case for the underlying stock. Without this discipline the buyer of options will make little headway overall. It is not enough simply to alight upon a volatile share and haphazardly choose a particular option series over a time scale of three, six or nine months. While it is more than likely that the shares will display some volatility before expiry of the option, the premium cost is high and the risks of success remote. A decision must be taken on the degree of optimism felt for the course of the underlying stock. The measurement of this optimism will largely determine which option series to select.

While the temptation remains to secure high gearing and incredible potential returns on capital employed by courtesy of the heavy, out-of-the-money series, a policy based wholly and indiscriminately on this strategy is unlikely to show any consistent gains: the odds are too heavily stacked against. Nevertheless, the out-of-the-money option is an alluring prospect to the bullish investor, as the volume figures often reveal. Because of this, the in-the-money options are sometimes neglected and downgraded as 'also-rans' when compared with their more glamorous relative. This can be a short-sighted and unsophisticated approach to the task in hand. Pedestrian (by comparison) the performance of the in-the-money option might be but, at times, it can have a most valuable and profitable role to play which should not be despised. (In the world of options it is unusual to use a word like 'pedestrian' to describe performance. While the performance gap between the out-of- and the in-the-money options can often make the latter look more than a little sluggish, the disparity between the performance of the in-the-money option and the underlying share can be equally startling.) At this juncture it might be useful to examine some of the occasions when the in-the-money series offers good value and is the 'right' option to select in the circumstances.

(A) *Purchasing a partly paid equity*

As the heavy, in-the-money option is often neglected by the buyers, the time value in the premium cost (i.e. premium less intrinsic value) can get too cheap, particularly for a high beta share. The astute investor contemplating a purchase of the underlying share may discover an attractive alternative financial proposition through the medium of the in-the-money option series. This can be the case if the shares have suffered a set-back in the market following a previously strong performance. The investor is thus purchasing effectively a partly paid equity, paying but a small time premium for the privilege. He can exercise into the underlying share at any time up to the expiry of the option, retaining the balance of the consideration proceeds in the interim: in a period of high interest rates the bulk of the cash placed in the money market will more than compensate for the time premium paid over the offer price of the share in the market. Should the shares rise in value the investor has covered the rise cheaply through his option: in-the-money options (particularly with a short time to expiry) will rise point for point with the underlying shares. The investor will have secured a large percentage return on capital employed and, totally relaxed about the situation, can review his strategy before deciding finally whether to exercise into the shares and take them up, or simply to sell the options and take the profit.

Example

Racal. 4 July 1980

Stock price (p)	Option series	Price (p)	Time value
264	Aug. 200	66	2
	Aug. 220	46	2

Available initial strategies
(1) Purchase the shares at 264 and take them up on account day.
(2) Purchase the same number of August 200 or August 220 options at 66 or 46 respectively and, just prior to expiry, exercise through them into the underlying shares. In the interim, deposit the balance of the consideration proceeds in the money market on seven days' call.

Available subsequent strategies
  (1a) Sell the shares at 302 on expiry day (27 August).
  (2a) Sell the options (Aug. 220) at 82* on expiry day (27 August).
  (3a) Exercise into the underlying shares by calling the Aug. 220 options, and sell the shares at 302 on expiry day (27 August).

The mathematics of the situation works out as follows.
  (1) Purchase, say, 50,000 Racal at 264:

Consideration	£132,000.00
T/S (Transfer stamp)	2,640.00
Commission	698.00
VAT	104.70
C/S (Contract stamp)	0.60
CSI (Council for the Securities Industries levy)	0.60
Outstanding total	£135,443.90

  (2) Purchase 50 contracts Aug. 220 at 46:*

Consideration	£23,000.00
Commission	405.00
VAT	60.75
C/S	0.30
CSI	0.60
Outstanding total	£23,466.65

*Since the time value is the same (i.e. two points) for the August 200 and the August 220 options, the latter becomes the obvious choice for the purposes of this exercise.

The mathematics of available sale permutations are as follows.
  (1a) Sell 50,000 Racal at 302 on 27 August (expiry day)

Consideration	£151,000.00
Commission	774.00
VAT	116.10
C/S	0.30
CSI	0.60
Proceeds received	£150,109.00

(2a) Sell 50 contracts Racal Aug. 220 at 82 on 27 August (expiry day).

Consideration	£41,000.00
Commission	585.00
VAT	87.75
C/S	0.30
CSI	0.60
Proceeds received	£40,326.35

(3a) Exercise through the Aug. 220s purchased at 46 into the underlying shares.
  (i) Purchase 50,000 Racal at 220.

Consideration	£110,000.00
T/S	2,200.00
Commission	610.00
VAT	91.50
C/S	0.30
CSI	0.60
Consideration	£112,902.40
Plus Cost of original option (2)	£ 23,466.65
Total consideration	£136,369.05

  (ii) Sell 50,000 Racal at 302 (27 August) as above.

Consideration	£151,000.00
C/S	0.60
CSI	0.60
Profits = Proceeds received	£150,998.80*
Less Total consideration	£136,369.05
Profit on transaction	£ 14,629.75

*Since the shares are sold within the same Stock Exchange account in which the options are exercised, the sale is classed as 'closing' and therefore no commission is payable.

These calculations, including the interest factor where applicable, are summarised in Table 3.5.

Table 3.5

Date: Friday 4 July 1980. Position: 50,000 Racal

Purchase shares at 264p	Purchase 50 RCL Aug. 220 at 46p		
Cost £135,443.90 payable 21.7.80	Cost	£ 23,466.65	payable 7.7.80
	Add	£ 153.44	interest (17%) lost over 2 weeks
		£ 23,620.09	
	Subtract	£ 2,583.73	interest (17%) on £112,902.40 (see (3a)) for 7 weeks
		£ 21,036.36	
	Add proceeds for exercise	£112,902.40	
		£133,938.76	
Total cost £135,443.90	Total cost £133,938.76		

Date: Wednesday 27 August 1980

Sold shares at 302p

Realising £150,109.00 received 8.9.80

Sold 50 Aug. 220 at 82p

Realising £40,326.35 received 28.8.80

Profit on transaction £14,665.10

Return on capital employed (7 weeks) 10.8%

Return on capital employed (annualised) 80.4%

Profit on transaction

(a) No allowance made for interest:

Cost	£ 23,466.65
Realised	£ 40,326.35
Profit	£ 16,859.70

Return on capital employed
            (8 weeks)   71.8%

Return on capital employed
            (annualised)   466.7%

(b) *Allowance made for interest on option monies:

Cost	£ 23,620.09	(includes lost interest £153.44)
Realised	£ 40,326.35	
Plus 10 days' interest	£ 187.82	
Profit	£ 16,894.08	

Return on capital employed
            (8 weeks)   71.5%

Return on capital employed
            (annualised)   464.7%

*Interest on the proceeds required for exercise into the shares (i.e. £2,583.73) has been excluded from these calculations.

Observations and result

A purchase of 50,000 Racal ordinary shares would have put at risk £135,443.90 to produce a profit of £14,665.10 (a return on capital employed of 10.8%).

A purchase of 50 Racal August 220 contracts would have put at risk £23,466.65 to produce a profit of £16,859.70 (a return on capital employed of 71.8%). The balance of the proceeds required eventually to exercise into the underlying shares (£112,902.40) was not put at risk and earned interest of £2,583.73, a figure which I excluded from the final profit calculation.

The in-the-money option clearly works out to be far more profitable than the purchase of the underlying security.

(B) *Use of in-the-money options for short-term trading*

It can sometimes happen, particularly following a short-term reaction in the price of a strongly performing share, that certain in-the-money option series are priced too cheaply. The eagle-eyed investor may well occasionally spot such an anomaly in a high beta share with considerable time value remaining in the option.

Example

Grand Metropolitan shares rose strongly (from 120 to 165) in the May/November 1980 equity rally. An inevitable retracement/consolidation subsequently took place, and by mid-August the share price had slipped back to 157; the 22 October in-the-money options had drifted down to levels where the time value was clearly too low with over two months outstanding before expiry (see Table 3.6(a)).

To achieve maximum gearing from this situation the October 140s were the obvious series to select. Within two weeks the bid prices on the shares had

Table 3.6

Date	Stock offer price (p)	Option series	Option offer price (p)	Time value
(a) 15.8.80	157	Oct. 120	39	2
		Oct. 130	29	2
		Oct. 140	19	2

Date	Stock bid price (p)	Option series	Option bid price (p)	Time value
(b) 27.8.80	165	Oct. 120	48	3
		Oct. 130	38	3
		Oct. 140	28	3

risen to 165 and the option prices had been transformed. The underlying share price rose by 5.1%; the October 140 option improved by 47.4% (see Table 3.6 (b)). Nothing more needs to be said!

(C) *Short-term trading approaching option expiry*

For short-term traders, in-the-money options approaching expiry are often an attractive alternative to dealing in the underlying stock over several Stock Exchange accounts. If a bullish view is taken of the underlying shares, it is often possible to deal via an in-the-money option, paying no more than a small time premium over the offer price of the underlying shares in the market. Substantial gearing can be achieved, particularly if strict comparison is made by investing an equal money sum in both the underlying stock and the option in question. The examples of the January 1980 option series (23 January expiry) given in Table 3.7 will illustrate the point.

Table 3.7

Stock	Date	Stock price (p)	Option series	Option price (p)	Date	Stock price (p)	Option series	Option price (p)
CGF	7.1.80	413	Jan. 260	155	21.1.80	480 (up 16%)	Jan. 260	220 (up 42%)
			Jan. 280	135			Jan. 280	200 (up 48%)
			Jan. 300	115			Jan. 300	180 (up 56%)
			Jan. 330	85			Jan. 330	150 (up 76%)
			Jan. 360	55			Jan. 360	120 (up 118%)
			Jan. 390	26			Jan. 390	90 (up 246%)
CTD	7.1.80	72	Jan. 70	3½	21.1.80	78 (up 8.3%)	Jan. 70	9 (up 157%)
CUA	7.1.80	134	Jan. 130	6	21.1.80	146 (up 8.9%)	Jan. 130	17 (up 183%)
GMH	7.1.80	129	Jan. 120	10	21.1.80	140 (up 8.5%)	Jan. 120	24 (up 140%)
M & S	7.1.80	78	Jan. 70	9	21.1.80	93 (up 19%)	Jan. 70	24 (up 166%)

In the examples in Table 3.7 the time premium (exercise price plus option price less stock price) paid for the privilege of purchasing gearing through the in-the-money series ranged from one point (M & S and GMH) to three points (CGF Jan. 390), the disparity reflecting simply the anticipated volatility differential of the individual shares. The gearing achieved in these examples is quite startling!

Finally, there are sometimes opportunities to be found in the price structure of the new, infant, in-the-money option (i.e. where the previous out-of-the-money option has been transformed into an in-the-money option by virtue of a sharp rise in the underlying share price). In circumstances where this strong price movement is generated by specific, public news or evidence, the fact that it is considered unlikely that the rise can now continue apace may be sufficient to reduce the time value element of the option price quite considerably. This process is sometimes overdone and thus presents a buying opportunity.

Example

On 13 May 1980 (after the close of business at 3.30 p.m.) Shell announced that they had made a huge Norwegian gas find. Table 3.8 traces the movement of the share price and the SHL July 360 options. Before the news was released, Shell's share price was 355 and hence the July 360 options were out-of-the-money with just over two months' life left before expiry.

Table 3.8

Date	Stock closing price at 3.30 p.m. (p)	July 360 closing quote at 3.30 p.m. (p)	
12.5.80	355	21–24	
13.5.80	356	21–24	
14.5.80	386	34–37	(Highest day's quote 40–43)
15.5.80	381	27–30	
16.5.80	375	23–26	
19.5.80	368	20–23	

On 13 May the July 360 series, four points out-of-the-money (share price 356), was quoted 21–24. Within four, admittedly volatile, trading days the option was eight points in-the-money (share price 368) and the quote was only 20–23. This was a somewhat illogical price and reflected an attempt to frustrate existing 'bull' positions in a highly volatile share following a strong move in the underlying share *after* an important announcement had been made.

To the continuing bulls of Shell it offered a golden opportunity for another 'bite at the cherry'. When the option expired on 23 July, Shell had advanced to 424; the July 360 quote was 61–64.

Choice of expiration period

Once the decision has been made to purchase an in-the-money call option and the series has been chosen, it remains for the time scale required for the option to become profitable to be selected. While this decision must be determined largely by the nature of the bull case for the underlying security, there are a number of general guidelines which should assist the investor.

(1) Almost any analysis of the volume figures in virtually any bull phase will reveal that most trading takes place in the short

options, i.e. those of the earliest expiration date. The reasons for this relate primarily to the high gearing provided by the lower prices of the options as the time values are smaller. The highest volume is often to be found in the moderate- to low-priced options with an exercise price close to, or just above, the prevailing share price – it is simply an exercise in generating gearing. Also, as I have discussed, time works against the buyer of options; he must rely on volatility. While lack of volatility is not a problem (in modern stock markets), nevertheless a clear feature of bull phases over the past few years has been their relatively short duration. This factor favours the short expiry option.

(2) By the same token, however, the longer options will be less volatile than their shorter counterparts. If the decision reached determines that a particular share may enjoy a slow, consistent growth rather than experience an explosive rise over the short term, then, undoubtedly, one of the longer duration options will be the correct choice. The time value paid will, of course, be higher, but, by definition, it will shrink less, particularly in the early months of the option life. Remember that time values disappear most rapidly in the final months of the option life: as much as one half of the original time value may be lost in the final two or three months.

(3) Dividends. The incidence of periodic dividend announcements can often affect the choice of which time period is chosen. An impending heavy, ex-dividend adjustment can add considerably to the effective cost of an already expensive, short-duration option; the consequent mark down of the underlying security price to accommodate the net dividend will have an immediate effect on the short-option premium, whereas the price of a nine-month option will be affected far less dramatically.

The varying price of time

It is difficult to be too dogmatic about the cost of buying time three, six or nine months forward. The choice of time scale will be influenced largely by the magnitude of expectation for either a market move as a whole or an individual share in particular: from therein beta valuation will be a powerful determinant of price differential between option series. Obviously the cost of buying time over a six- or nine-month horizon will be higher than the valuation placed upon a three-month period of expiration. The longer options, however, will rarely command a price of twice and three times respectively the cost of the short option. A look at the time values (expressed as a percentage of the underlying share price) of various options listed on six shares, both before and after a sharp rise in the market, may be useful at this juncture as an indication of the cost of purchasing time (see Table 3.9). I have taken the period from early November 1979 to the end of January 1980 (FTI rose from 406 to 450) and highlight in each case both the in-the-money (ITM) and the out-of-the-money (OTM) series which straddled the then-prevailing underlying share price.

Table 3.9

	Early November 1979				*End of January* 1980			
			Time value				*Time value*	
	Share	*Time*	*% share price*		*Share*	*Time*	*% share price*	
Share	*price (p)*	*scale*	*ITM*	*OTM*	*price (p)*	*scale*	*ITM*	*OTM*
BP	374	3	5.1	4.0	336	3	6.8	7.4
		6	7.5	7.0		6	12.5	10.7
		9	13.4	N/A		9	14.3	13.1
CGF	312	3	3.5	7.1	448	3	7.4	9.2
		6	7.7	8.7		6	12.3	13.8
		9	9.3	10.9		9	17.0	18.5
GMH	134	3	6.7	5.6	137	3	6.6	6.6
		6	10.4	8.2		6	10.9	11.7
		9	N/A	14.2		9	17.5	16.8
GEC	319	3	5.0	5.6	359	3	6.1	8.6
		6	8.8	9.4		6	11.1	13.6
		9	12.9	13.8		9	15.0	17.5
CTD	82	3	6.1	3.7	75	3	7.3	6.7
		6	11.0	8.5		6	10.0	9.3
		9	13.4	11.0		9	12.0	11.3
ICI	333	3	5.7	2.1	377	3	4.2	4.2
		6	7.2	3.9		6	7.1	7.4
		9	11.7	7.5		9	10.3	9.8

A number of observations can be made from Table 3.9: I must caution, however, that few of them may be taken as rules of thumb, applicable religiously in each and every comparable situation.

The three best share performances from the list were CGF, GEC and ICI, in that order. On any historical beta analysis up to this point, only GEC would have commanded a high valuation. CGF had begun to perform strongly only over the previous twelve months, while ICI's relative price performance over the years would rarely have warranted a high beta factor – the November undervaluation of its out-of-the-money options (in comparison with the other two) over the three-, six- and nine-month time scales underlines this 'fact'. Following a sharp rise in the market, particularly where the time scale is short, there is a natural tendency for option time values to expand: the above figures reveal quite clearly that this is almost a common factor throughout the list, even for those shares which failed to perform with the market (BP, GMH and CTD).

Why should this apparent contradiction be so? Explanations will vary between the individual stocks in question: don't search for a common theme since one rarely occurs. In BP's case, for example, the historic relative price action of the shares would not have permitted a high beta valuation; however, BP was one of the strongest share performers in the 1979 pre-election bull market and, as a result, its option time values had expanded considerably and remained high during the period under review (which covered the Government's offer for sale of 80 million ordinary shares at 363p). The case of GMH necessitates a different explanation. The high time valuations for the options reflected the fact that GMH shares traditionally respond well to a general upward move in the market and thus rank in the high volatility group. Their disappointing performance (134p to 137p) in the period under review was considered historically freakish and totally out of character: time values thus started high and expanded with the market rise in true textbook fashion. This 'unusual' price performance from GMH was a clear warning that all was not well and presented a golden opportunity to write the short options. (The share price subsequently fell to 120 before rebounding to 165 in the June/July rally.) The high time values accorded the CTD options both before and after the market rise defy rational explanation, on the grounds of both historical price performance and apparent future prospects. Admittedly, the shares did enjoy a brief flurry later in the year, but it was all over very quickly and, by September, the shares had dropped to 60p while the FT Index had risen almost 100 points. The option valuations ruling in the November–January review simply presented the sellers with a golden opportunity, of which, judging from the low volume figures, few people took advantage.

ICI's share performance and the response of its options to this provide another varied, interesting case. The low November valuation of the out-of-the-money options (over all three time periods) highlights the low beta rating of the shares as was discussed earlier. The 44-point (13%) rise in the share price over the period was as untypical in its relative strength as GMH's performance was in its relative weakness. The move had little credibility (in option measurement) and thus the in-the-money values contracted. Although the out-of-the-money rates expanded from their very low comparative levels in November, they still remained significantly cheaper than any of the other five under scrutiny.

The question is often posed as to whether high or low time valuations after a strong general market rise give any indication of future trends? The answer, unhappily, cannot be a definite 'yes' or 'no' right across the board. The generalisations that can be made may be summarised as follows.

(1) If a high volatility share performs poorly in a strong market and option time values remain high, it will *probably* present a suitable writing opportunity, but one cannot be totally relaxed about it and the time scale chosen could be crucial.

(2) If a low volatility share performs poorly in a strong market move and option time values remain high, one can be reasonably relaxed about the writing opportunities presented.

(3) A strong move (relative to the market) in a high volatility share and an expansion of option time values across the board on some occasions can signal a further sharp move in the shares. This is best illustrated by the example of CGF in the November–January rally. The rise in the share price from 312p to 448p was accompanied by an expansion of time values (particularly the out-of-the-money series) to levels that looked desperately expensive – a 4.2% time value for a three-month, out-of-the-money option (36.8% annualised) after a sharp rise in the share price can certainly not be considered cheap! Nevertheless, within two weeks the share price had risen from 448p to over 500p (on the back of the now infamous 'dawn raid') and the options took off once again.

(4) A strong move relative to the market in a low beta share coupled with an expansion of time values should be treated warily. Unless a compelling case can be made for further progress in the stock or the market as a whole, it is best left alone since history is not on your side!

41

(5) A strong move relative to the market in a low beta share coupled with a contraction of time values will sometimes offer a further attractive buying opportunity but, once again, caution should be exercised. The case of ICI discussed earlier illustrates this development: here, the contraction of time values after the strong share performance offered a suitable opportunity to capitalise upon the impending two-week rise in the price from 377p to 402p.

We can now return to the central theme of this discussion, namely which option expiry period to choose in order to accommodate the bull case for a particular share. It goes without saying that, if the expectations are for slow, consistent growth in the share price rather than for short-term fireworks, the problem is easier and the longer time scale should be selected. Regrettably for this line of argument, modern market movements in high beta shares are usually violent and of relatively short duration. What happens therefore to the short and the longer options as the share price swings about wildly? To what extent do the heavier time premiums of the longer options mitigate against their price performance during a sharp, short-term, upward move in the underlying share price? An analysis of such a sharp move in the CGF share price between June and July 1980 will illustrate the problem admirably. Table 3.10 traces the movement of the Consolidated Gold-fields shares from 497 to 561 and back to 524 in just four trading weeks. The corresponding performances of the relevant in-the-money and out-of-the-money options series over the short (July (A)), medium (October (B)) and long (January (C)) time scales are recorded. The percentage figures in brackets monitor the rise in each case from (A) to (B) and from (A) to (C).

The following observations can be made about the data in Table 3.10.

(1) The most spectacular gains were achieved in the short expiry (July) series on the back of the move in the share price from 497 to 561 (A to B). The progression from an 85% increase in the heavy in-the-money options (July 420) to a gain of 550% in the heavy out-of-the-money series (July 550) is perfectly consistent with the theory of gearing. The behaviour of the October and January series also reveals a 'correct' profit progression, illustrating quite clearly the effect of a sharp, short-term price movement on the longer options.

Table 3.10

	A	B		C	
	23 *June*	7 *July*	(A−B%)	23 *July*	(A−C%)
Stock price (p)	497	561	(+12.9%)	524	(+5.4%)
Options					
July 420	80	148	(+85%)	104	(+30%)
July 460	47	108	(+130%)	64	(+36%)
July 500	19	68	(+258%)	24	(+26%)
July 550	4	26	(+550%)	Nil	(−100%)
Options					
Oct. 460	75	135	(+80%)	95	(+27%)
Oct. 500	49	102	(+108%)	63	(+29%)
Oct. 550	25	63	(+152%)	34	(+36%)
Options					
Jan. 460	90	145	(+61%)	95	(+5.6%)
Jan. 500	65	115	(+77%)	77	(+18.5%)

(2) The pull-back in the share price from 561 to 524 by 23 July (expiry day) obviously took heaviest toll of the short, out-of-the-money series (July 500s and 550s). A month earlier an investor sensing a short-term rise in the underlying shares would have found the geared attractions of the July 500s and 550s more compelling than their in-the-money counterparts. However, with the shares standing at 497 and only one month remaining to expiry, the out-of-the money series were hardly cheap at premiums of 19 and 4 respectively. A more conservative investor might have sought less gearing and a lower effective time value through the July 460s, already 37p in-the-money. His prudence would have been rewarded subsequently with a 130% gain in the option between A and B and a 36% gain from A to C. The more aggressive purchase of the two out-of-the-money series would have received justifiably greater rewards (258% and 550%) while the shares powered upwards, but suffered dramatically as the share price faltered (in the case of the July 550 series, it ended its life worthless). Of course, it is easy to job backwards with the benefit of hindsight but, unless the ultra-short-term case for buying the shares was overwhelming, the July 550s were too far out-of-the-money within the outstanding time left to expiry to rank as anything other than an outrageous speculation.

Occasionally, the gamble will pay off handsomely but, more often than not, the net result will be total loss of capital committed if the option is left to the bitter end. The October 550 series at 25p looked far better 'value' and offered the luxury of a four-month time scale. A 152% gain from A to B may pale into insignificance when compared with the 550% achievement of its younger 'brother'. At the end of the day (23 July), however, while the latter was dead and worthless, the former had achieved a 36% return on capital employed in a month, with plenty of time outstanding for further developments. In cases similar to this one, the longer options will usually be the more sensible acquisition.

Out-of-the-money series

The CGF example that I have just analysed leads quite naturally in to a more detailed consideration of out-of-the-money option series, without doubt the almost inevitable choice of the speculator pursuing the gearing multiplier or the fortune hunter chasing the prospect of untold wealth just around the corner through astronomic returns on capital employed. Early in January each year it is always fascinating to view the list of the best performing shares of the previous twelve months: the list will inevitably include companies whose shares have risen several hundred per cent over the period, achieved by virtue of a market re-rating of a medium-size company, or a take-over bid, or the result of an obscure tea or rubber company being used as a 'shell' operation by the latest property whizz kid or ambitious financier. Encouraging and reassuring as these situations may be to the ever-hopeful investment die-hards, they are usually the preserve of a tiny minority of knowledgeable people and, for the rest of us, they are not easy to capitalise upon until, at best, a lot of the action is over. Also, without knowing precisely what is going on, they are often 'one-way', restricted markets, posing quite severe problems of liquidation once the trend changes; as such, they must be considered high-risk investments.

The really marvellous thing therefore about traded options is that, although there will always be a restricted list of option stocks, barely a quarter of the year goes by without one or several examples of a super-growth investment materialising on the back of leading shares. It is almost a contradiction in terms to envisage the prospect of huge returns on capital employed by courtesy of ICI or CTD, but it happens periodically; the high volatility growth stocks offer the same prospect

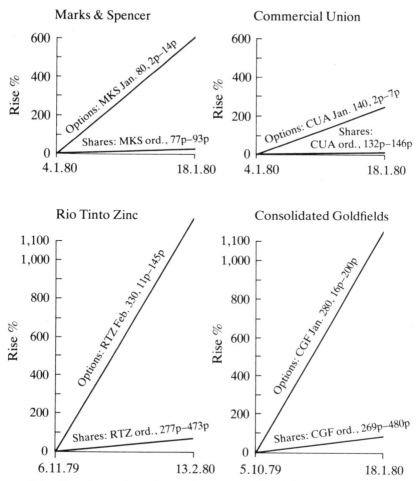

Figure 3.1. Graphs to show the performance of M & S, CUA, RTZ and CGF shares and options, end of 1979 to beginning of 1980.

regularly! The examples for the three years since the traded option market opened its doors in London in Figure 3.1 and Table 3.11 illustrate my point.

Bearing in mind that the stock market tends to spend more time falling than rising (the upward moves are sharp and of short duration), and also that time is no ally of the option buyer, could it not be argued (as many American textbooks on the subject maintain) that purchases of out-of-the-money options are as high a risk investment as is, for example, the annual attempt to spot next year's stock market winners which I earlier mentioned? The answer, as is often the case in option matters, is 'yes' and 'no'. It is 'yes' if the investor pursues an

Table 3.11

Stock	Rise in stock (dates)		% gain	*Option series	Option increase over same time scale		% gain
1978							
LSI	221 (24/7)	to 238 (7/8)	8	Oct. 240	4	to 10	150
GMH	109 (4/9)	to 121 (14/9)	11	Oct. 110	5	to 14	180
EMI	143 (2/10)	to 163 (9/10)	14	Nov. 160	4	to 13	225
GEC	276 (31/7)	to 333 (14/9)	21	Oct. 280	15½	to 57	268
1979							
GEC	308 (7/11)	to 343 (11/12)	11	Jan. 330	5	to 23	360
BP	857 (3/11)	to 954 (6/12)	11	Jan. 950	6	to 28	367
LSI	221 (10/11)	to 253 (9/1)	14	Jan. 240	3	to 14	367
RTZ	226 (2/1)	to 264 (19/1)	17	Feb. 260	2	to 12	500
CGF	178 (12/1)	to 198 (24/1)	11	Jan. 180	2	to 18	800
1980							
RCL	226 (27/5)	to 290 (21/7)	28	Aug. 260	7	to 30	329
LSI	321 (27/6)	to 366 (21/7)	14	Jul. 353	1½	to 14	833
BP	336 (1/9)	to 459 (23/10)	36	Oct. 390	5	to 70	1,300
GEC	344 (2/6)	to 488 (18/7)	42	Jul. 390	3½	to 98	2,700

*All out-of-the-money series.

undisciplined policy orientated to purchasing short-expiry, heavy out-of-the-money options, on high beta stocks at random, with scant regard either to whether the market as a whole is over-bought or over-sold, or in the erroneous belief that an option is cheap simply because it is offered in single figures. (Indeed, far from being cheap, an option offered in single figures is likely to be horribly expensive, as a quick calculation of its annualised cost will reveal.) The answer is 'no' if out-of-the-money option purchases are used intelligently to 'gear' up a balanced, deliberate investment decision where an attempt has been made to 'measure' the bullish expectations for the stock in question. How often one reads that the conservative investor will choose the in-the-money option series (deriving comfort from the intrinsic value already achieved) leaving the wild speculator to fund his out-of-the-money 'gamble'! Without actually stating it, the innuendo always is that the former is safer than the latter. The reader will discover just how safe and comforting the in-the-money option is if he gets his investment decision wrong; as the share price drops, the option will follow suit on almost a point-for-point basis. In these circumstances there is much greater risk of extensive capital loss through the 'safe' in-the-money series than in its 'speculative' out-of-the-money counter-part.

When to buy out-of-the-money options – general rules

Do *not* buy out-of-the-money options unless the following are true.

(1) Expectations are for a significant percentage rise in the under-lying stock in question or the market as a whole. Even after a heavy fall in share prices, out-of-the-money option premiums are unlikely to be considered statistically cheap; this will leave the decision regarding the choice of which expiry date to select to a matter of individual judgement at the time.

Example

Table 3.12

GEC June 1980				*GEC 23 July* 1980 (*expiry of July series*)			
Share price	402			Share price	473		
Option prices	July	420	8	Option prices	July	420	53	(+563%)
	Oct.	420	24		Oct.	420	72	(+200%)
	Jan.	420	39		Jan.	420	94	(+141%)

The sharp percentage rise (18%) in GEC's share price from 402 to 473 generated a progression of option increases ranging over the balance of the three-, six- and nine-month expiry dates from 563% to 141%. Once again, this is perfectly consistent with the textbook theory, the heavy gearing in the short-expiry option (July 420) commanding most of the action and attention and subsequently turning in the goods with a spectacular price performance. Without prior knowledge of just how well received the GEC results were likely to be – the relative weakness of the share price over the preceding months offered little guidance on this score and might easily have led the investor to take the opposite view – the July 420 options, costing eight points with a strike price 6% out-of-the-money with only 23 days left to expiry, by no stretch of the imagination could be considered cheap. The October 420 series hardly looked too exciting either, once again 5% out-of-the-money and cost-ing 6% additionally in time value. As I suggested earlier, normal in-vestment prudence in such circumstances must dictate a heavier orientation towards the longer expiry date (i.e. October 420). GEC's results were far better than the stock market analytical forecasts had projected and the shares took off en route to 555 before expiry of the October options.

(2) On the assumption that there is a reasonable time left to expiry (not in the last few weeks of an option life), out-of-the-money options can be purchased to accommodate a rally in the price of a share without it necessarily developing into a significant percentage rise. The out-of-the-money option series will be extremely sensitive and responsive to such moves and it is not uncommon to witness a near 100% move in the option relative to a 5% movement or less in the underlying stock. The examples in Table 3.13 will reveal just how sensitive out-of-the-money options are to sharp moves in the underlying stock, even where the latter never attains the strike price of the option.

Example

Table 3.13

Land Securities: end of January 1980			Shell: end of January 1980		
		April 300			April 360
Stock offer		option offer	Stock offer		option offer
price (p)	Date	price (p)	price (p)	Date	price (p)
286	21.1.80	18	331	21.1.80	18
275	22.1.80	11	325	22.1.80	11½
279	23.1.80	14	325	23.1.80	10
281	24.1.80	17	332	24.1.80	13
286	25.1.80	18	340	25.1.80	20
			350	28.1.80	27

Shell: mid-May 1980			
		July 360	
Stock closing		option closing	
mid. price		mid. price	
3.30 p.m. (p)	Date	3.30 p.m. (p)	
355	12.5.80	22½	
356	13.5.80	22½	
386	14.5.80	35½	Day's high 41½
381	15.5.80	28½	
375	16.5.80	24½	

The Shell (mid-May) example in Table 3.13 brings out a number of interesting general points.

(a) Shell announced that they had made a huge Norwegian gas find after the market had closed (3.30 p.m.) on 13 May 1980. Before the official opening of the Stock Exchange the next day, Shell's share price had touched 400 in brokers' inter-office dealings. By the time the option market had opened at 9.45 a.m. the share price had reacted to 385; the opening quotation of the option was 40–43 which subsequently turned out to be the day's high. Movements of this magnitude in the underlying stock, rare though they may be, highlight the case for opening the Traded Options Market at 9.30 a.m. each (business) day.

(b) When the price of Shell was 355 (12 May) the price of the July 360 option was 22½; four days and considerable price gyration later (16 May) the shares stood at 375 (+20) while the option (now 15 points in-the-money) was only two points better. As the July series had reasonable time left to expiry, the option price structure was clearly wrong (too cheap) and offered continuing bulls of the stock another golden opportunity. (By 23 July the stock had risen to 424 and the option had almost trebled.)

(c) As a general rule, restrict purchases of out-of-the-money options to high beta stocks.

(d) When purchasing heavy out-of-the-money options in antici-pation of a market rise or rally, restrict purchases to high beta stocks as in (c) with a reasonable time left to expiry, but, in so doing, spread the risk and do not expect to succeed each time. No high-profit/high-risk investment ever does! For example, towards the end of August 1980, continuing bulls of the market following the initial June/July upsurge had the choice of buying both BP Oct. 390 (stock price 360) and GMH Oct. 180 (stock price 160) at 4.5 points premium. On the evidence of their relative price performance up to that point, GMH appeared to have more potential than BP. However, a bid for the Coral Group put paid to the prospect of any financial success for the Oct. 180 series, while the Iran/Iraq confrontation helped the BP Oct. 390 series to achieve a fifteenfold appreciation within the life of the option.

Finally, for those who wish to dream of achieving the ultimate in gearing concepts and the financial multiplier effect that goes with it, I will close this section with the following strategy.

If the investor can envisage a substantial rise in the underlying share price of a volatile stock listing a traded option, the strategy involves purchasing the short out-of-the-money option, so long as it has a reasonable time left to expiry. As the share price moves up and a new out-of-the-money series is introduced, immediately close (by selling) the existing bull position and re-invest the same sum in the new out-of-the-money series, i.e. 'walk-up' the series. Pursue the strategy ruth-lessly until the judgement is made that the share price has run its course or that expiry of the series is too imminent to render continuation of the strategy a sensible proposition. In this instance, if it is adjudicated that the share price has plenty of mileage left in it, simply move into the out-of-the-money series with the next expiry date. Dreams can become a reality in the traded options market: over the past three years there have been numerous examples where this strategy could have been implemented satisfactorily. The single example in Table 3.14 of Shell early in 1979 will suffice to illustrate the theme and whet the appetite! How to turn £1,000 into £138,000 in just four months!

Table 3.14

Share price (p)	Date	No. of contracts	Option series	Option price (p)	Purchase cost (£)	Proceeds realised (£)
560	29.1.79	+18	April 600	5½	990	
610	8.2.79	−18	April 600	23		4,140
	8.2.79	+69	April 650	6	4,140	
651	8.3.79	−69	April 650	15		10,350
	8.3.79	+207	April 700	5	10,350	
700	20.3.79	−207	April 700	8		16,560
	20.3.79	+414	April 750	4	16,560	
759	*2.4.79	−414	April 750	20		82,800
	2.4.79	+230	July 800	36	82,800	
804	4.5.79	−230	July 800	60		138,000

*The April options were to expire on 18 April hence the move into the July series.

SETTLEMENT OF BARGAINS RESULTING FROM EXERCISE

The London Stock Exchange system of account settlement is based on a dealing period of ten days, beginning on a Monday and ending on the Friday of the following week, although, due to the incidence of public holidays, minor variations occur in this timetable. It is essential that there is at least one business day remaining in the account period in order that transactions resulting from the exercise of an option may be cleared. Therefore an option may be exercised on any business day during its life with the exception of the last dealing day of an account. Expiry dates for options will usually fall on the second Wednesday of the last complete dealing period within the expiration month.

A traded option may normally be exercised up to 5 p.m., but exercise notices for any class will be accepted until 6 p.m. on the date of expiry of a series. The exercise of an option will be assigned by a computerised, random selection process to a holder of an open, written position of the same series. This will be effected after the positions have been updated for the day's transactions. The day following the submission of the exercise notice the broker will issue to the exerciser (buyer) a contract note stating that he has purchased x thousand shares of XYZ Co. at (strike price) pence per share and the assignee's (seller) broker will issue a contract note stating that he has sold the same. Settlement will be on the account day of the dealing period then ruling, for example dealings for 15–26 September 1980 inclusive would have been settled on 6 October 1980: if an option was exercised on, say, 17 September the resulting purchase/sale would have been settled on 6 October. In other words, the bargain has become a straightforward Stock Exchange transaction and, as such, may be 'closed' within the dealing period: a buyer may sell his shares and the seller may buy back his position. Once an assignment notice has been received by the writer of an option contract, he may not close his position in the option market but must provide the shares called, either by surrendering his existing holding or by purchasing the equity in the market. If the shares are purchased to meet assignment within the account period, there is no transfer stamp liability on the purchase transaction.

It should be noted that, while a buyer of an option contract cannot exercise his option until the day after the day of purchase (as he will not have paid for the contract until then), the writer of an option contract may be advised that an assignment notice has been received from LOCH against his position on the day following his written transaction.

4

Spreads and hedges, part I

From the heady, almost rarified atmosphere of the out-of-the-money option series, it is now time to turn our attention to the undoubtedly less glamorous but nevertheless useful function that *spread* techniques can offer in the implementation of a bull strategy. Technically, a spread involves the simultaneous purchase of one call option with the sale of another on the same underlying security: the two calls may differ as to either exercise price or date of expiry or both. Various combinations and permutations are permissible within the theory, the dominating factors being primarily the investment objectives to be achieved and the collateral regulations required within the rules. At its most basic, the overriding motivation for a spread is defensive, i.e. a hedge; it sacrifices part of the potential profit from an option purchase for the protection from incurring a substantial loss.

BASIC BULL SPREADS

A bull spread (also termed a money, price or vertical spread) is achieved by combining two call options with a common expiration date and differing exercise prices. By purchasing a call with a lower exercise price and selling a call with a higher exercise price, the object of the exercise is to reduce the cost of purchase between one third and one half (and this also reduces the appreciation in the underlying security needed to produce a profit). We can now consider three examples of simultaneously opened bull spreads in anticipation of a large percentage rise in the underlying share price, a smaller rise in the underlying share price and a technical rally in a poorly performing stock.

(1) *A large percentage rise in the underlying share price*

Between the end of May 1980 and the expiry of the July option series (23 July), the GEC share price rose from 348 to 473 (36%).

Date	Middle price (p) Stock	Offer price (p) July 360	Bid price (p) July 390
27.5.80	348	14	3

An investor anticipating a rise in the GEC stock price from 348 but not exceeding 393 decided to open up the GEC July 360–390 bull spread ten times (by buying ten contracts of the July 360 at 14 and simultaneously selling ten contracts of the July 390 series at 3; thus, he was paying 11 points for the spread. The cost of the transaction, allowing for all expenses, works out as shown in Table 4.1.

Table 4.1

Purchase 10 GEC July 360 at 14		= £1,400 (*opening transaction*)	Sell 10 GEC July 390 at 3		= £300 (*opening transaction*)
Comm. 10 × 1.50	15.00		Comm. 10 × 1.50	15.00	
Comm. 2.5%	35.00		Comm. 2.5%	—	
VAT	7.50		VAT	2.25	
Contract stamp	0.30		Contract stamp	0.30	
	£57.80	£1,457.80		£17.55	£282.45

Total net cost £1,457.80 − £282.45 = £1,175.35.

The following observations can be made to date.

(a) The net cost of the above transaction is the difference between the two premiums (11 points) plus expenses. A profit will be made if the share price exceeds 371 (360 + 11) by expiry of the option. The shares can rise to 390 before the July 390 series has any intrinsic value; beyond 390 the loss on the July 390 offsets any gain on the July 360 series and no further profit can be achieved.

(b) By exercising both sides of the spread simultaneously, the commission charges relating to the sale of the July 390 option are reduced under the spread concession rule (see section on commission and charges). This concession is granted on the sale contract up to five days after (and including) the date of purchase of the bull part of the spread. While it is thus possible to

53

execute only the purchase side of an intended spread strategy first, in the hope that the price of the underlying security might rise over the five days and accordingly improve the bid price of the sale transaction (i.e. the higher strike price series), it does carry the considerable risk that the share price might drop and thus frustrate the original spread terms. In the case of GEC above, this risk might well have been considered an acceptable one: with almost two months outstanding to expiry of the July series it was unlikely that the bid of 3 for the July 390 series would have been threatened, even with a weakened share price, over the ensuing few days. Nevertheless, executing only one side of an intended spread in the hope of later improving the terms (in the jargon of the option market 'lifting a leg') does carry considerable risks where high beta stocks are concerned and is not to be recommended as a general rule, particularly where a close watch on movements of the stock and the options is not practical.

To continue the GEC example: by the morning of the expiry day of the July series (23 July), the GEC share price had surged to 475. The prices of the relevant options were as follows.

Date	*Middle price (p)* Stock	*Bid price (p)* July 360	*Offer price (p)* July 390
23.7.80	475	114	86

The spread had to be closed, either by exercising into the July 360 series and being assigned against in the July 390 series, or by simply selling the July 360 at 114 and buying the July 390 at 86, thus receiving a credit of 28 points. The mathematics of the transactions, allowing for all expenses, work out as shown in Table 4.2.

Table 4.2

Sell 10 GEC July 360 at 114		= £11,400 (*closing transaction*)	Purchase 10 GEC July 390 at 86		= £8,600 (*closing transaction*)
Comm. 10 × 1.50	15.00		Comm. 10 × 1.50	15.00	
5,000 × 2.5%	125.00		5,000 × 2.5%	SC*	
5,000 × 1.5%	75.00		3,600 × 1.5%	SC*	
1,400 × 1.0%	14.00				
VAT	34.35		VAT	2.25	
C/S	0.30		C/S	0.30	
CSI levy	0.60		CSI levy	0.60	
	£264.25	£11,135.75		£18.15	£8,618.15

Table 4.2 – *cont.*

Net return £11,135.75 − £8,618.15 = £2,517.60	
Net cost	= £1,175.35
Net profit	= £1,342.25

*SC = Spread concession.

Further observations can be made from Table 4.2.

(c) A straightforward purchase of the July 360 at 14 (27.5.80) and a sale at 114 at expiry (23.7.80) would have produced a profit of over 700%. While the profit from the spread (115%) pales into comparative insignificance, it is easy to be critical with the benefit of hindsight. When the shares stood at 348, the best projection at that time was a rise to 390 within the life of the option; the spread thus had some merit in reducing the effective cost of the straight bull position. With respect, no investor should complain about a defensive strategy that necessitates no further action or attention while the share price is rising and produces a net gain of 115% over two months, compared with the 36% (gross) rise in the underlying security itself.

(d) Nevertheless, for those who remain dissatisfied with the relative performance of the spread and whose reassessment of the price performance of the share as it passed through the 390 target levels demanded a less conservative stance, it is always possible to disrupt the spread (this way) by buying back the sale of the July 390 series. This would leave the July 360 clear and running, able to take almost a point-for-point benefit from the further rise in the share price to the expiry day peak of 473. Once again, flexibility of action remains of paramount importance in any strategy involving traded options.

(2) *A smaller percentage rise in the underlying share price*

Land Securities' share price move over the same time scale provides an example of a simultaneously opened bull spread over a smaller percentage rise in the underlying share price.

Date	Middle price (p) Stock	Offer price (p) July 330	Bid price (p) July 360 ·
13.5.80	333	19	6½

The investor projecting a rise in the underlying security not exceeding 366½ opens up the July 330–360 bull spread by purchasing the July 330 at 19 and selling the July 360 at 6½ for a debit of 12½. The net cost of the operation is calculated in Table 4.3.

Table 4.3

+ 10 LSI July 330 at 19		=£1,900	− 10 LSI July 360 at 6½		=£650
Comm. 10 × 1.50	15.00		10 × 1.50	15.00	
1,900 × 2.5%	47.50		650 × 2.5%	S/C	
VAT	9.38		VAT	2.25	
C/S	0.30		C/S	0.30	
	£72.18	£1,972.18		£17.55	£632.45

Total net cost £1,972.18 − £632.45 = £1,339.73

By expiry of the July option series (23.7.80), LSI shares had risen to 363. A rights issue valuation of 7 points had reduced the strike prices of the July 330 and July 360 to 323 and 353 respectively.

Date	Middle price (p) Stock	Bid price (p) July 323	Offer price (p) July 353
23.7.80	363	38	10

The investor closed out the spread by selling the July 323 at 38 and buying the July 353 at 10, i.e. selling the spread for 28 points. The net figure involved is worked out in Table 4.4.

Table 4.4

− 10 LSI July 323 at 38		=£3,800	+ 10 LSI July 353 at 10		=£1,000
Comm. 10 × 1.50	15.00		10 × 1.50	15.00	
3,800 × 2.5%	95.00		1,000 × 2.5%	S/C	
VAT	16.50		VAT	2.25	
C/S	0.30		C/S	0.30	
	£126.80	£3,673.20		£17.55	£1,017.55

Net return £3,673.20 − £1,017.55 = £2,655.65
Net cost   = £1,339.73

Net profit   = £1,315.92   i.e. 98% return on capital employed (RCE).

Although 3.5 points were lost on the July 353 series, the return on capital employed via the spread (98%) outpaced the straight purchase and sale of the July 323 series (86%) and compared most favourably with the gross (9%) profit from the movement in the underlying stock.

(3) *A technical rally in a poorly performing stock*

A bull spread may be a useful tactic in an endeavour to reduce the exposure of a straight option bull purchase in a situation where there is no strong case for buying the shares in the short term, but where a rally is considered a strong possibility within the life of the option and the risk : reward ratio of the spread is thus acceptable. The Courtaulds example below illustrates this.

Date	*Middle price (p)* Stock	*Offer price (p)* July 70	*Bid price (p)* July 80
1.5.80	69	5	2

In anticipation of a possible rise in the share price above 80, the July 70–July 80 bull spread is opened at a cost of three points. The net figures (for 10 contracts once again) are shown in Table 4.5.

Table 4.5

+ 10 CTD July 70 at 5		= £500	− 10 CTD July 80 at 2		= £200
10 × 1.50	15.00		10 × 1.50	15.00	
500 × 2.5%	12.50		200 × 2.5%	S/C	
VAT	4.13		VAT	2.25	
C/S	0.30		C/S	0.30	
	£31.93	£531.93		£17.55	£182.45

Net cost £531.93 − £182.45 = £349.48.

Loss of this amount was considered an acceptable risk in relation to the possible maximum gain of 10 points (i.e. difference between the two strike prices) if the share price exceeded 80 before expiry of the option. The strategy was successful and, by early July, the share price had rallied strongly to 87.

Date	*Middle price (p)* Stock	*Bid price (p)* July 70	*Offer price (p)* July 80
7.7.80	87	16	8½

The spread could now be closed by selling the July 70 option at 16 and purchasing the July 80 series at 8½ (see Table 4.6).

Table 4.6

− 10 CTD July 70 at 16		=£1,600	+ 10 CTD July 80 at 8½		=£850
10 × 1.50	15.00		10 × 1.50	15.00	
1,600 × 2.5%	40.00		850 × 2.5%	S/C	
VAT	8.25		VAT	2.25	
C/S	0.30		C/S	0.30	
	£63.55	£1,536.45		£17.55	£867.55

Net return £1,536.45 − £867.55 = £668.90
Net cost   = £349.48

Net profit   = £319.42   i.e. 91% RCE

By the expiry of the July series just over two weeks later, the CTD share price had collapsed to 68p and, as a result, both the July 70 and the July 80 series expired worthless. If no action had been taken when the underlying share price had achieved its target objective, a maximum loss would have resulted for the spread. The moral of the example is obvious!

Turning a straight option bull position into a bull spread

The RTZ example given below illustrates how a straight option bull position may be turned into a bull spread.

A bullish view was taken on RTZ in late May 1980:

	Middle price (p)	Offer price (p)
Date	Stock	Aug. 420 series
27.5.80	355	8

Ten contracts of the August 420 are purchased at 8. By mid-June the price of RTZ has risen to 405. The August 420 series have responded in true, positive, 'out-of-the-money' fashion and are now 18 bid. At this point the investor, while still bullish, begins to feel a little nervous of a pull back in the share price. He has three available options:

(1) to do nothing,
(2) to sell at 18 and take 10 points profit, or
(3) since the Aug. 460 series are standing at 8 bid, he can open up the Aug. 420–460 bull spread by selling the Aug. 460 at 8.

The investor decides on the third course of action and has thus achieved a 'spread Utopia', having purchased the spread for nothing (+ Aug. 420 at 8, − Aug. 460 at 8). He has thus recouped his original capital outlay (which can be used for additional option purchases if required) and stands to benefit from any further rise in the share price to a maximum of 40 points (i.e. the difference in the strike price 460 − 420 = 40).

At expiry of the August series (27 August) the position is as follows.

Date	Middle price (p) Stock	Bid price (p) Aug. 420	Offer price (p) Aug. 460
27.8.80	471	49	13

The spread can be closed either by exercising into the Aug. 420 series and having the Aug. 460 assigned against, or simply by selling the Aug. 420 at 49 and buying back the Aug. 460 at 13, thus selling the spread for 36. The mathematics work out as shown in Table 4.7, allowing for all expenses. No further comment should be necessary!

Table 4.7

+ 10 RTZ Aug. 420 at 8		=£ 800	− 10 RTZ Aug. 460 at 8		=£800
10 × 1.50	15.00		10 × 1.50	15.00	
800 × 2.5%	20.00		*800 × 2.5%	20.00	
VAT	5.25		VAT	5.25	
C/S	0.30		C/S	0.30	
	£40.55	£ 840.55		£40.55	£759.45

*No spread concession.

Net cost £840.55 − £759.45 = £81.10.

− 10 RTZ Aug. 420 at 49		=£4,900	+ 10 RTZ Aug. 460 at 13		=£1,300
10 × 1.50	15.00		10 × 1.50	15.00	
4,900 × 2.5%	122.50		S/C	—	
VAT	20.63		VAT	2.25	
C/S	0.30		C/S	0.30	
	£158.43	£4,741.57		£17.55	£1,317.55

Net return £4,741.57 − £1,317.55 = £3,424.02
Net cost   = £   81.10

Net profit   = £3,342.92

HORIZONTAL BULL SPREADS

A *horizontal* or *calendar* bull spread involves the simultaneous sale of a short (i.e. near-expiry) call and purchase of a longer dated call with the same exercise price. For example:

Date	Stock	Stock price (p)	Bid price (p) Oct. 390	Offer price (p) Jan. 390
End September 1980	LSI	380	7	34

Horizontal spread = sell Oct. 390 at 7 and buy Jan. 390 at 34.

As expiration of the October series approaches, the time value of the October options will waste more rapidly than the January series and the profit on the spread accrues as the difference between the two calls widens.

Most successful calendar spreads require neutral price expectations for the underlying stock over the remaining life of the expiring option; ideally, the expiring option will waste to zero as the stock price remains slightly below the exercise price. The relatively low time values available in the low beta stocks are usually safer territory for calendar spreads than their high time value/high volatility counterparts.

Where short-term, neutral expectations prevail for a high beta stock it is often possible to use the calendar spread as a ploy to reduce the cost of the longer bull position particularly via the out-of-the-money series. If the share price remains static or drifts lower, the near-expiry call will end up worthless (without incurring the expense of buying it back) while the longer option should not drop much in value. The effective cost of the longer option is thus lowered by the amount the near-expiry call has wasted. If the underlying share price rises (against expectations), the near option will still lose its time value faster than the longer call: if a loss is sustained in buying back the near option, the longer option should have moved up proportionately, more than recouping any loss on the short sale.

Investors would be well advised to restrict their activity in calendar spreads to the out-of-the-money series, particularly in the early days of trial and error. Calendar spreads effected in the at-the-money or in-the-money series run the distinct risk of early assignment of the near-expiry call, thus terminating and frustrating the spread potential.

Example

The investor, bullish for the Racal share price over the medium term, saw little to go for in the short term towards the end of July 1980. He contemplated a horizontal spread in the out-of-the-money series.

Date	Middle price (p) Stock	Bid price (p) Aug. 300	Offer price (p) Nov. 300
21.7.80	289	7	22

The spread was effected by selling the Aug. 300 at 7 and buying the Nov. 300 at 22. If the share price remained marginally below 300 over the ensuing month, the Aug. 300 option would expire worthless, while the Nov. 300 would be little changed; he would thus have achieved a reduction of seven points (less expenses) on the effective cost of his longer Nov. 300 bull position. At expiry of the August series (23.8.80), the Racal share price had risen to 300 and the August 300 expired worthless.

Date	Middle price (p) Stock	Offer price (p) Aug. 300	Bid price (p) Nov. 300
23.8.80	300	Nil	27

The result of a perfectly executed calendar spread was an effective cost of 15p (22 − 7) for the Nov. 300 series which could either be run as a straight bull position or be sold at 27. If the latter course is adopted, the mathematics of the transaction work out as shown in Table 4.8, allowing for all expenses. The £1,006.47 net profit represents a return on capital employed of 63% over one month. Not bad for a defensive option strategy!

Table 4.8

21/7 + 10 RCL Nov. 300 at 22	=£2,200		21/7 − 10 RCL Aug. 300 at 7	=£700
10 × 1.50	15.00		10 × 1.50	15.00
2,200 × 2.5%	55.00		S/C	—
VAT	10.50		VAT	2.25
C/S	0.30		C/S	0.30
	£80.80	£2,280.80	£17.55	£682.45

Net cost £2,280.80 − £682.45 = £1,598.35

23/8 − 10 RCL Nov. 300 at 27	=£2,700
10 × 1.50	15.00
2,700 × 2.5%	67.50
VAT	12.38
C/S	0.30
	£95.18
	£2,604.82

Net return	=£2,604.82
Net cost	=£1,598.35
Net profit	=£1,006.47

DIAGONAL, VARIABLE-RATIO AND BUTTERFLY SPREADS

Before I move on to consider the strategies available for writing options, I will briefly outline the structure of and conditions suitable for implementing *diagonal*, *variable-ratio* and *butterfly* spreads. Unless and until the investor has had some considerable experience in executing the more 'traditional' spreads and has the interest and the time to monitor share and option price movements on a daily basis, he would be well advised to use the following spreads infrequently and with considerable caution.

Diagonal bull spreads

A diagonal spread differs from a calendar spread in that the simultaneous purchase and sale of two call options combines different strike prices *as well as* different expiry dates. The investor, bullish over the medium term for a particular stock, may look to execute a diagonal spread, which usually involves the purchase of a longer dated (i.e. six- or nine-month) at-the-money option series and the sale of the short-dated out-of-the-money options series.

(1) If the short-expiry option wastes to zero over its remaining life, the investor will have achieved a reduction in the effective cost of his longer dated bull position.

(2) The longer dated at-the-money option series is considered good collateral/cover for writing the short-expiry option.

(3) The time value on the written, short expiry, out-of-the-money option is unlikely to be particularly high and will thus give little protection for a sharp drop in the underlying share price. Accordingly, diagonal spreads should be effected only where price expectations for the share price range from neutral to mildly bearish.

Variable-ratio bull spreads

The investor who is dissatisfied with the relatively low downside protection offered by the diagonal spread will consider a variable-ratio bull spread. As the highly geared out-of-the-money series offers limited protection during a sharp fall in the underlying share price, the investor will look to the deep in-the-money series for his written position: he will simultaneously buy a *number* of the mildly out-of-the-money or at-the-money options to accommodate his option upside objectives from a rise in the share price.

(1) The variable ratio (of bull position to bear position) will generally be a minimum of $3:1$. If the share price falls, the theory is that the profit from the one written in-the-money option will cover the loss on the three bought options. If the share price rises, the heavier gearing via the at-the-money series should produce a higher profit than the loss incurred in buying back the in-the-money bear position.

(2) The sale of a deep in-the-money option and the purchase of an at-the-money option with similar expiry dates requires cash cover to the value of the difference between the two strike prices.

Example: British Petroleum

Share price (p)	Bid price (p) Oct. 300	Offer price (p) Oct. 360
360	70	36

An investor executes a variable-ratio bull spread by selling one contract of the Oct. 300 series at 70 and simultaneously purchasing three contracts of the Oct. 360 series at 36. Not allowing for expenses, the calculations work out as shown in Table 4.9.

Table 4.9

	£
Sell one Oct. 300 at 70	700
Cash collateral required (i.e. difference in strike prices 360–300)	600
Net credit	100
Purchase three Oct. 360 at 36	1,080
Net consideration	980

(3) As the share price moves up and down, either side of the spread can be terminated to accommodate a changed investment decision. However, if the investor gets more bearish and closes (by selling) his bull position (i.e. three contracts Oct. 360), he will be left with a straight bear position via his sale of one contract of the Oct. 300 series. Without any compensating bull position the

63

collateral rules for an uncovered writer will then be applicable: a substantial injection of cash will be required to run the bear position (see the section on uncovered writing).

(4) If the underlying share price stays static or moves within a tiny trading range, the spread will show a loss.

(5) The sale of a deep in-the-money option runs the considerable risk of being exercised early, particularly if the underlying stock goes ex dividend within the time scale of the spread: if this were to happen the spread would be disrupted, offering little chance of a profitable outcome.

Butterfly spreads

Finally, the butterfly spread involves three calls with equally spaced exercise prices and a common expiry date: the butterfly is effected by a purchase of the low and the high exercise price options and a sale of the intermediate series in the ratio of 1:2:1.

Example: Grand Metropolitan

Date	Stock price (p)	Oct. 120 Offer price (p)	Oct. 130 Bid price (p)	Oct. 140 Offer price (p)
6.6.80	137	23	16	10

The GMH butterfly is achieved by:
+ 1 Oct. 120 at 23 (OP)
− 2 Oct. 130 at 16 (OP)
+ 1 Oct. 140 at 10 (OP).

(1) The difference between the purchase and the sale transactions (23 + 10 − 32) is one point: this (plus the expenses involved in opening and closing the butterfly) is the *maximum* loss sustainable on the transaction, regardless of the underlying share price level at expiry.

(2) The maximum gain from the GMH butterfly will occur if the share price closes at 130 (the intermediate strike price) on expiry of the October options. If this occurs, the October 130 sale will expire worthless (+32, i.e. 2 × 16), as will the October 140 series (−10); the October 120 option will have an intrinsic value of 10, thus involving a loss of 13 (23 − 10). This leaves a credit of nine points on the spread, less the original cost of one point, less the expenses relating to four option transactions (three opening and one closing).

(3) The margin requirements for the butterfly spread can be ex-

plained more easily if it is analysed as a combination of a bull spread (buy the Oct. 120 and sell the Oct. 130), and a bear spread (sell the Oct. 130 and buy the Oct. 140) which I will consider in greater detail later. The bull spread requires no further margin since the Oct. 120 provides good cover for the Oct. 130. The bear spread requires as margin the difference between the two strike prices involved (Oct. 130 and Oct. 140, i.e. 10).

(4) The chances of achieving maximum profitability from a butterfly spread are remote: common sense dictates that the butterfly spread should be used sparingly.

5

Expenses, dividends and capital changes

COMMISSION AND OTHER CHARGES

As with all transactions conducted on the floor of the London Stock Exchange, the commission charged is governed by the rates laid down in the *Rules and Regulations of the Stock Exchange.*

For option transactions the rates charged are the same for buying and selling call or put options. Unlike traditional options, the commission for traded options is calculated on the option money consideration and *not* on the value of the underlying security. The rates are currently:

£1.50 per option contract (usually covering 1,000 shares)
plus 2.5% of the first £5,000 option money consideration,
    1.5% on the next £5,000 option money consideration,
    1% on any excess option money consideration.

For commission purposes, business in the same series may be amalgamated for five business days, including the first day of dealing. Should an option position be closed within the five business days, only the £1.50 per contract should be charged; the *ad valorem* (the 'percentage' portion of the commission) is waived. However, all bargains are subject to minimum commissions, these being £10.00 overall with £5 minimum attributable to the *ad valorem* portion of the total commission. When dealing in a 'spread' position, the half of the transaction with the lower option money consideration is charged the £1.50 per contract fee, while the full commission is payable on the other (heavier) half of the deal. This is known as a spread concession (SC).

The other charges made for option transactions are VAT, contract stamp and the CSI levy.

VAT: For United Kingdom and EEC residents VAT is charged at 15% on the commission levied. For a non-resident no VAT is applicable.

66

Contract stamp: This is the only charge that is calculated on the under-lying security. For option transactions half the usual rates apply, as follows.

Value of the underlying security	Usual rate (p)	Option contract rate charged (p)
In excess of £100 but not exceeding £500	10	5
In excess of £500 but not exceeding £1,500	30	15
In excess of £1,500	60	30 (maximum)

CSI levy: On all Stock Exchange transactions with £5,000 consider-ation involved, a charge of 60p is levied. This is a contribution to the financing of the Committee for the Securities Industry.

The commission rules and charges are easier to comprehend when applied to specific transactions, as the following examples should show. Take a United Kingdom resident dealing in IMP Nov. 80 option series at a premium of 4½p. The costs of the transactions involved in pur-chasing different numbers of contracts are calculated below.

If he purchases one contract:

Consideration	1 × 1,000 × 4½p			£	45.00
Commission	1 × £1.50	£ 1.50			
	2.5% of £45	£ 1.13			
		£ 2.63	(since this is below £10.00, the minimum commission is charged)	£ 10.00	
VAT 15% of £10.00				£ 1.50	
Contract stamp – underlying consideration 1,000 at 80p = £800.00			(below £1,500)	£ 0.15	
			Total charges £ 11.65	£	11.65
			Total cost	£	56.65

If he purchases four contracts:

Consideration	4 × 1,000 × 4½p			£	180.00
	4 × £1.50	£ 6.00			
	2.5% of £180	£ 4.50*			
		£ 10.50			
*Since the *ad valorem* is below the £5.00 minimum the commission charged is £6.00 + £5.00 = £11.00				£ 11.00	
VAT 15% of £11.00				£ 1.65	
Contract stamp – underlying consideration 4,000 at 80p = £3,200 (in excess of £1,500)				£ 0.30	
			Total charges £ 12.95	£	12.95
			Total cost	£	192.95

If he purchases 10 *contracts:*

Consideration	10 × 1,000 × 4½p			£ 450.00
Commission	10 × £1.50	£ 15.00		
	2.5% of £450	£ 11.25		
Total commission		£ 26.25	£ 26.25	
VAT 15% of £26.25			£ 3.94	

Contract stamp – underlying consideration 1,000 at 80p
= £8,000 (in excess
of £1,500) £ 0.30

Total charges	£ 30.49	£ 30.49
Total cost		£ 480.49

If he purchases 100 *contracts:*

Consideration	100 × 1,000 × 4½p			£ 4,500.00
Commission	100 × £1.50	£150.00		
	2.5% of £4,500	£112.50		
Total commission		£262.50	£262.50	
VAT 15% of £262.50			£ 39.38	
Contract stamp (underlying consideration in excess of £1,500)			£ 0.30	

Total charges	£302.18	£ 302.18
Total cost		£ 4,802.18

If he purchases 150 *contracts:*

Consideration	150 × 1,000 × 4½p			£ 6,750.00
Commission	150 × £1.50	£225.00		
	2.5% of £5,000	£125.00		
	1.5% of £1,750	£ 26.25		
Total commission		£376.25	£376.25	
VAT 15% of £376.25			£ 56.44	
Contract stamp (underlying consideration in excess of £1,500)			£ 0.30	
CSI levy (consideration in excess of £5,000)			£ 0.60	

Total charges	£433.59	£ 433.59
Total cost		£ 7,183.59

If he purchases 250 *contracts:*

Consideration	250 × 1,000 × 4½p			£11,250.00
Commission	250 × £1.50	£375.00		
	2.5% of £5,000	£125.00		
	1.5% of £5,000	£ 75.00		
	1% of £1,250	£ 12.50		
Total commission		£587.50	£587.50	
VAT 15% of £587.50			£ 88.13	
Contract stamp (underlying consideration in excess of £1,500)			£ 0.30	
CSI levy (consideration in excess of £5,000)			£ 0.60	

Total charges	£676.53	£ 676.53
Total cost		£11,926.53

The calculations are the same for both sellers and buyers of traded options. Thus, if the client is a seller of the same option positions, the proceeds for a sale of one contract would be £33.35 (£45.00 − £11.65) and the proceeds of a sale of 250 contracts would be £10,573.47 (£11,250.00 − £676.53).

Commission on exercise of an option

(1) *Buyers*
1.5% on the first £7,000 consideration (number of shares × price).
0.5% on the next £93,000 consideration.
Thereafter at the rates laid down in Section C of Appendix 39 of the Rules and Regulations of the Stock Exchange.
(2) *Writers, on assignment*
0.75% on the first £7,000 consideration.
0.25% on the next £93,000 consideration.
Thereafter at one half of the rates laid down in Section C of Appendix 39 of the Rules and Regulations of the Stock Exchange.

Concessions

(1) *Aggregation*
Bargains in the same series for the same principal may be aggregated on the day of the first bargain and on the four subsequent business days for the purpose of charging commission.
(2) *Five-day closing rule*
Where a 'closing' transaction is carried out on the day of the opening bargain or on one of the four subsequent business days, a broker is permitted to receive the option money portion of the minimum commission charge. In such instances, however, the fixed charge of £1.50 per option contract must still be applied.

Using the examples of one contract and 250 contracts of IMP Nov. 80 series purchased at 4½p, the cost of closing the transactions within the five-day dealing concessionary period and after can be calculated (see Table 5.1). It has been assumed for the calculations that the option positions can be sold at 6p.

Following on from the calculations in Table 5.1, the mathematics for spread transactions would be as shown in Table 5.2.

Table 5.1

One contract IMP Nov. 80 sold at 6p

		Within 5 days	Outside 5 days
Consideration	1 × 1,000 × 6p	£ 60.00	£ 60.00
Commission	1 × £1.50	£ 1.50	
Consideration	1 × £1.50		£ 1.50
Commission	2.5% of £60		£ 1.50
ad valorem waived		nil	
Total commission		£ 1.50	
Below minimum, therefore £10 charged			£ 10.00
VAT 15% of £1.50		£ 0.23	
VAT 15% of £10.00			£ 1.50
Contract stamp		£ 0.15	£ 0.15
Net proceeds		£ 58.12	£ 48.35

250 contracts IMP Nov. 80 sold at 6p

		Within 5 days	Outside 5 days
Consideration	250 × 1,000 × 6p	£15,000.00	£15,000.00
Commission	250 × £1.50	£375.00	£375.00
Commission	2.5% of £5,000		£125.00
ad valorem waived		nil	
	1.5% of £5,000		£ 75.00
	1% of £5,000		£ 50.00
Total commission		£375.00	£625.00
VAT 15% of £375.50		£ 56.25	
VAT 15% of £625.00			£ 93.75
Contract stamp		£ 0.30	£ 0.30
CSI levy		£ 0.60	£ 0.60
Net proceeds		£14,567.85	£14,280.35

+ 10 contracts Racal Nov. 300 at 35
− 10 contracts Racal Nov. 330 at 14

$$\frac{\quad}{21}$$

i.e. the spread has been purchased for 21.

+ 10 contracts at 35p

Consideration 10 × 1,000 × 35p		£3,500.00
Commission 10 × £1.50	£ 15.00	
2.5% of £3,500	£ 87.50	
	£102.50	
Total commission		£ 102.50
VAT 15% of £102.50		£ 15.38
Contract stamp		£ 0.30
		£3,618.18

− 10 contracts at 14

Consideration 10 × 1,000 × 14p		£1,400.00
Commission 10 × £1.50	£ 15.00	
ad valorem waived	nil	
Total commission	£ 15.00	£ 15.00
VAT 15% of £15.00		£ 2.25
Contract stamp		£ 0.30
		£1,382.45

Cost

Net cost of purchasing spread = £2,235.73.

− 10 RCL Nov. 300 at 32
+ 10 RCL Nov. 330 at 16

$$\frac{\quad}{16}$$

i.e. the spread has been sold for 16.

− 10 contracts at 32p

Consideration 10 × 1,000 × 32p		£3,200.00
Commission 10 × £1.50	£ 15.00	
2.5% of £3,200	£ 80.00	
	£ 95.00	
Total commission		£ 95.00
VAT 15% of £95		£ 14.25
Contract stamp		£ 0.30
		£3,090.45

+ 10 contracts at 16p

Consideration 10 × 1,000 × 16p		£1,600.00
Commission 10 × £1.50	£ 15.00	
ad valorem waived	nil	
Total commission	£ 15.00	£ 15.00
VAT 15% of £15.00		£ 2.25
Contract stamp		£ 0.30
		£1,617.55

Net proceeds of selling spread = £1,472.90.

N.B. When selling this spread, a margin requirement of £3,000.00 is needed (+ 330p − 300p = 30p Dr. × 10 × 1,000 = £3,000).

TREATMENT OF DIVIDENDS

This is an important subject for both buyers and writers of options and is often misunderstood by the enthusiastic 'amateur'.

The holder of a traded option contract is *not* entitled to receive any payment of dividend declared on the underlying security unless he has exercised the option *before* the underlying security has been made 'ex dividend' (i.e. marked down by the net amount) by the Stock Exchange. In other words, the holder of a traded option contract must become the beneficial owner of the underlying shares represented by the option before the ex-dividend adjustment is effected. While no amendment is made to the actual terms of the traded option contract as a result of an ex-dividend adjustment, the price of the option will reflect the change in the underlying share price as it is marked down.

As a general rule shares are adjusted 'XD' of the first day (usually Monday) of a Stock Exchange account period. Traded options, on the other hand, may not be exercised on the last day of an account, and thus option prices have accommodated the impending 'XD' mark down by the last day of the previous account. This is particularly noticeable in companies like ICI, for example, who tend to announce their results and dividend on the first Thursday of a Stock Exchange account and go 'ex dividend' on the first Monday of the next account. The example involving ICI in Table 5.3 will illustrate the point quite clearly.

Table 5.3

ICI figures announced 28.2.80. Final dividend net 11.0p. XD 10.3.80

6.3.80		7.3.80		10.3.80		
Share price (p)	391	Share price (p)	387	Share price (p)	371	XD
Apr. 360	32	Apr. 360	22	Apr. 360	21	
Apr. 390	14½	Apr. 390	11	Apr. 390	9½	
Apr. 420	9	Apr. 420	6	Apr. 420	5	

Other companies, like GMH for example, usually have a longer time lag between the announcement of their figures and the ex-dividend declaration. In this case, the option premiums take a longer period to adjust and on the Friday prior to the Monday ex-dividend declaration there is little change in the option prices, as the GMH example in Table 5.4 shows.

Table 5.4

GMH interim figures announced 10.6.80. Interim dividend net 2.88p. XD 11.8.80					
7.8.80		8.8.80		11.8.80	
Share price (p)	152	Share price (p)	154	Share price (p)	153 XD
Oct. 140	13½	Oct. 140	16	Oct. 140	15½
Oct. 160	5	Oct. 160	6	Oct. 160	6
Oct. 180	2	Oct. 180	2½	Oct. 180	2½

ADJUSTMENT FOR CAPITAL CHANGES IN THE UNDERLYING SECURITY

(1) Share capitalisation issue

Upon any allotment of fully paid shares in the underlying security (by way of capitalisation of profits or reserves to members of the company issuing the underlying security), the terms of all the series of the options then currently listed on that underlying security will be adjusted so that the product of the unit trading and the exercise price will be the same after the allotment as it was before the allotment (see the example in Table 5.5).

Table 5.5

Shell Transport & Trading Company Limited 1 for 1 capitalisation issue ex date 4.6.79		
(Friday) 1.6.79	SHL ordinary shares 761p	
	750 options July 53	Dealing unit: 1,000 shares
	Oct. 70	
	Jan. 102	
(Monday) 4.6.79	SHL ordinary shares 378p	
	375 options July 25	Dealing unit: 2,000 shares
	Oct. 34	
	Jan. 49	

The dealing unit will remain at 2,000 shares on existing options until expiry. When the new options with different expiry dates are introduced the dealing unit reverts to the customary 1,000 shares (i.e. in the case of Shell in Table 5.5, April 1980 onwards).

(2) Rights issue

When an offer by way of rights on an underlying security is made to holders of that security, or in the event of the holders of an underlying security becoming entitled to any rights or benefits other than those mentioned above, the Stock Exchange will fix a value for such rights or other benefits and the exercise prices of traded option series on that underlying security will be adjusted accordingly (see the example in Table 5.6).

Table 5.6

Land Securities Investment Trust Limited 1 *for* 6 *rights issue at* 263p ex date 11.6.80

(Tuesday) 10.6.80	LSI ordinary shares 314p		
	300 options July	19	Dealing unit: 1,000 shares
	Oct.	37	
	Jan.	49	

Valuations of rights as at close of business 10.6.80

Share price 314p	6 × 314p =	1,884p
	Rights consider-	
	ation =	263p
	Value of 7 shares	2,147p average price 307p

Therefore value of rights adjustment 7p per share
(314p − 307p)

(Wednesday) 11.6.80	LSI ordinary shares ex rights 313p		
	293 options		
	(300–7) July	25	Dealing unit: 1,000 shares
	Oct.	42	
	Jan.	55	

The dealing unit remains unchanged: 1,000 old shares. The buyer of the option has no entitlement to the 'new' shares, the strike price adjustment having compensated for the issue.

In certain instances and subject to specific conditions, partly paid ordinary shares have been permitted as alternative margin for traded call options.

(3) Take-overs

On the announcement of a take-over, the Council may decide to restrict the issue of new series and the writing of further option contracts.

Existing options will continue to represent the right to acquire non-assented stock. At a later stage, probably on a take-over becoming unconditional, the Council will rule on the rights and responsibilities of option holders and writers.

Example: EMI/Thorn

16.10.79. The board of Thorn Electric Industries Limited announce that they intend to make an offer for all issued ordinary capital of EMI on the basis of: for every 20 ordinary stock units of the company, 7 ordinary shares of 25p of Thorn.

15.10.79. EMI shares   95.   16.10.79. EMI shares   128.

Nov.	90	10	Feb. 90	18	May 90	24		
Nov.	100	6	Feb. 100	12	May 100	18		
Nov.	110	4	Feb. 110	NA	May 110	NA		

Nov.	90	42	Feb. 90	44	May 90	46
Nov.	100	32	Feb. 100	34	May 100	36
Nov.	110	22	Feb. 110	NA	May 110	NA

31.10.79. Council ruling: that when the offer document is issued, the following provisions apply in respect of EMI traded options:

(1) *Writers of EMI London traded options*
Writers of options will be required in the event of assignment to deliver EMI ordinary stock in 'non-assented' form, unless a request to assent accompanies the assignment notice.

(2) *Holders of EMI London traded options*
Holders of EMI London traded options hold only the right to acquire EMI stock in non-assented form, but upon exercise they may ask for a delivery in 'assented' form.

(3) *Exercise*
Upon exercise the normal rules governing the settlement of Stock Exchange bargains will apply and accordingly *at that stage* the exerciser may request delivery of 'assented' stock, in which event the assignee must use his best endeavour to make delivery in assented form.

6.11.79. EMI and Thorn Electric announce that they have reached agreement on the basis for a merger which EMI recommend to their holders. Terms of revised offer are: for every 100 ordinary stock units of 50p of EMI, 28 ordinary shares of 25p plus £58, 7% net convertible preference shares of Thorn.

6.11.79. EMI shares   145.

Nov. 90	47	Feb. 90	64	May 90	66
Nov. 100	37	Feb. 100	54	May 100	56
Nov. 110	27	Feb. 110 NA		May 110 NA

5.12.79. The announcement of the merger between Thorn and EMI becoming unconditional.

10.12.79. Council ruling:

. . . the following further provisions will apply to EMI London Traded Options:

Trading in options

- On 10 December 1979 EMI traded options will become a restricted class. No new open position will be permitted except for the account of a market maker or board dealer, and no further series will be created.
- Where no open position exists in an EMI series, the series will be cancelled.
- The EMI class will be finally withdrawn as a class of traded options on 28 May 1980 (i.e. the expiry of the May series) or at such earlier time as no open position exists in the class.

10.12.79. EMI shares 131.

Feb. 90	48	May 90 NA*	*Option closed, no open position.
Feb. 100	38	May 100 39	
Feb. 110	28	May 110 NA	

8.4.80. Council ruling: that, with effect from Monday 21 April 1980, assignments on EMI London traded options contracts must be satisfied by delivery of Thorn EMI Limited shares on the following basis:

for each EMI traded
  option contract

280 Thorn EMI ordinary shares of
  25p each *plus*
580 Thorn EMI 7% Convertible Redeemable second
  Cumulative Preference (1992–99) shares of £1 each.

6

Selling (writing) call options

COVERED OPTION WRITING – THE CONSERVATIVE APPROACH

This strategy will normally be adopted by the more conservative option writer against the cover of the underlying shares in his portfolio. The primary objectives of this policy are to generate cash flow 'receipts' of premium income in an attempt to improve the overall per annum return on the money invested or to 'insure' against an anticipated price decline, and to 'write down' book cost by premiums received less expenses. The premium thus represents the covered writer's compensation for relinquishing any appreciation in the share beyond the strike price on the upside and his measure of protection if the shares decline (see the Courtaulds example in Figure 6.1).

If the shares rise rather than fall, the writer may either buy in the option or surrender the underlying shares when the option is exercised. If the shares are bought back for a loss smaller than the amount of the premium received less expenses, a small profit will be made and the benefit retained of any further rise in the underlying shares. Before reaching a decision to buy in anticipation of a further rise in price, the investor should calculate how much further the shares need to appreciate to render buying back a profitable exercise. The covered writer thus has ample flexibility once he has implemented a particular investment decision. However, there are two important rules which affect this flexibility. Firstly, the option may be exercised and the writer called upon to deliver the shares at the strike price *at any time* during the option's life prior to expiration and regardless of the prevailing price of the shares. Secondly, once a writer has received an exercise

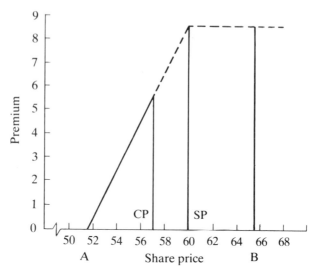

Figure 6.1. Graphical example of maximum profit/downside protection points: Courtaulds, September 1980. Share price = 57; October 60 series = 5½; CP = current price; SP = strike price; A = downside break-even point (57 − 5½ = 51½); B = point of maximum profitability (57 + 3 + 5½ = 65½).

notice from the Clearing Corporation *he may not close his position in the option contracts to which that exercise notice refers by a 'closing purchase transaction'*.

In rising markets writing covered options should be undertaken only by the conservative user willing to sell the underlying shares at a pre-determined price above the then-prevailing price of the shares. The investor is being offered a premium that, in all probability, will seldom exceed 10% of the share price over three months. Accordingly, he is limiting his upside potential. He is also somewhat limiting his overall flexibility. For example, if the shares suddenly decline sharply, he is protected on the downside by the premium less expenses. The price fall may well have unnerved him to the extent that he may wish to sell the underlying shares; should he do so he would automatically assume the role of the 'naked', uncovered writer with the inherent risk of the shares rebounding and rising over the exercise price within the remaining life of the option. He can still buy back the option, of course, if he fears this contingency, but in so doing he ceases to have any position either in the option itself or in the shares. Clearly, any decision to buy back an option can only be taken by the investor based upon his expectation of market movements at the time, coupled with the degree of risk he is willing to tolerate.

By now it should be clear that time is of paramount importance in option trading, both for the buyer and for the writer (seller). Over any long-term time scale, writing options is consistently more profitable than buying options. The reason is, quite simply, that time works to the advantage of the seller: if the underlying security moves in a narrow trading range, the option value will decrease to nothing as the expiration date approaches. 'In-the-money' options are made up of two component parts – an intrinsic value and a time value. As a general rule, the greater the time remaining before expiration, the greater the time value; as expiration approaches, the time value component of the option price 'wastes away' to zero or its intrinsic value.

Determining the best exercise price

Choice of which strike price to select is one half of the overall problem solved for the aspiring covered writer. Option time value is at its maximum when the share price equals the exercise price. Time value decreases as the share price rises above the exercise price or drops below it. The aspiring writer wishing to profit from attractive time values in general terms might execute his business according to the formula below:

neutral expectations for price movement – write 'at-the-money' options,

bullish expectations for price movement – write 'out-of-the-money' options,

bearish expectations for price movement – write 'in-the-money' options.

This formula represents the theoretical approach which tends to be highlighted in all the option textbooks. It could conceivably apply where the manager of funds is perfectly relaxed about the prospect of losing the underlying stock (through exercise of the option) at a predetermined price higher than the current market level. More often than not, however, investment management is rarely so black or white: the grey area usually predominates. Numerous fund managers and private investors with whom I have discussed the technique of covered option writing have been concerned primarily with the risk of losing the underlying security through option exercise at the strike price. This concern stems from:

(1) fear of increasing an already high liquidity level as a result of the options being called, and

(2) more important possibly, the desire to avoid the exposure of a large capital profit liable to incur a substantial tax charge.

These two points are of obvious importance: any covered writing programme must make due allowance for them. Accordingly, while the theoretical formula outlined above is too simplistic to be adopted as a general rule for all investors at all times, nevertheless the selection of strike price will be governed by an investment decision relating to the underlying security. Is the investor bullish, bearish or neutral in his expectation for the share? Once he has determined whether he is bullish and bearish he must then attempt to measure or quantify the degree of the stance taken. Traded options can be used to satisfy virtually any declared strategy; investment decision-making must be clear-cut and the investor must be clear-sighted in implementing this. As an example I will take three individual investors, A, B and C, who come to three separate conclusions about the likely future course of the GMH share price from a level of 150. They have the choice of four different January strike price options in endeavouring to implement their respective strategies.

Investor A. Neutral expectations: not unhappy to lose the underlying shares at somewhat higher than the present price, or alternatively to pocket a substantial premium.

Investor B. Bearish expectations: wishes to write an option giving maximum downside protection.

Investor C. Bullish expectations: wishes to write an option giving as high a potential sale price as possible for the shares.

	Option series *available*	*Premiums* *(bid price)*
(1)	GMH Jan. 130	29
(2)	GMH Jan. 140	21
(3)	GMH Jan. 160	7.5
(4)	GMH Jan. 180	4

Assume a price of 150 for GMH at expiry:

(1) Premium received 29. Underlying shares called at 159 (130 + 29).
(2) Premium received 21. Underlying shares called at 161 (140 + 21).
(3) Premium received 7.5. Underlying shares retained.
(4) Premium received 4. Underlying shares retained.

In this event, the choice of strike price for each of the three investors would have been as follows.

Investor A would have written (1) or (2), the Jan. 130 or Jan. 140 series.
Investor B would have written (1), the Jan. 130 series.
Investor C would have written (3) or (4), the Jan. 160 or Jan. 180 series.

Assume a price of 131 *for GMH at expiry:*

     (1) Premium received 29. Underlying shares called at 159 (130 + 29).
     (2) Premium received 21. Underlying shares retained.
     (3) Premium received 7.5. Underlying shares retained.
     (4) Premium received 4. Underlying shares retained.

Investor A would have sold his shares at 159 as in (1), or retained his shares and reduced his book cost by 21 points as in (2). Both cases would have achieved the desired result.

Investor B would have more than covered the fall in the share price by writing (1). He would have sold his shares at 159 (130 + 29).

Investor C would have got it wrong. He would retain his shares but would have reduced his book cost by either 7.5 or 4 points compared with a drop of 19 points in the share price over the period.

Assume a price of 181 *for GMH at expiry:*

     (1) Premium received 29. Underlying shares called at 159.
     (2) Premium received 21. Underlying shares called at 161.
     (3) Premium received 7.5. Underlying shares called at 167.5.
     (4) Premium received 4. Underlying shares called at 184.

Investor A would have achieved his objective, but he would have sold his shares at 159 compared with the prevailing price of 181: this is, however, a high-opportunity cost for the investor keen to maintain a shareholding in this company.

Investor B is in the same position as investor A, having totally misread the direction of the share price.

Investor C achieved his bullish expectations and was rewarded with the highest effective sale price through the Jan. 180 series at 184.

This simple exercise should reveal just how important it is for the investor to determine his view concerning the likely course of the underlying share price for the period under review. Once this has been done, the decision as to which strike price to adopt is largely self-determining. The success of the operation will depend almost entirely on the correctness or otherwise of the investment decision. Nevertheless, even if this decision proves totally wrong in the final analysis, the reader can rest assured that writing covered call options over a reasonable time scale not only will provide a new dimension to investment management, but also will be preferable and certainly more profitable than the alternative of simply sitting with the underlying shares.

Attaining an assured return is one of the basic prerequisites of selling covered calls, and thus the major risk is that the price of the underlying security may drop sharply. Hence, as a general rule, the investor pursuing the essentially conservative strategy of selling covered calls, where loss of the underlying security at a predetermined price is no problem, should sell the call with the lowest exercise price, preferably standing well below the prevailing share price to afford maximum downside protection. In a previous paragraph on the selection of which options to purchase I stressed that volatility of price movement was an important component. For covered writers the reverse is often an important requirement; the investor seeking to avoid exercise of his underlying shares should look carefully for reasonable premiums among the low beta shares.

Selecting the best expiry date

I maintained earlier that the choice of which strike price to select was one half of the covered writer's problem: the remaining half involves selection of the best expiry date.

At any one time, option valuations over a three-, six- or nine-month duration will vary between option classes; time values will also vary within an option class to reflect the level of exercise price (in-, at- or out-of-the-money). The example of LSI in Table 6.1, when the share price stood at 301 at the beginning of a full option cycle, will illustrate the point I wish to make.

Table 6.1

	Options		
	In-the-money	*At-the-money*	*Out-of-the-money*
Time scale	*Share price* 280	*Share price* 300	*Share price* 330
3 months (July)	45	29	16
6 months (Oct.)	55	41	27
9 months (Jan.)	66	54	42

In general terms, an at-the-money option over a six-month time scale will trade at around 1.5 times the valuation of a three-month option, whereas a nine-month call will command roughly twice the valuation of the shortest option. The valuation differential will be less marked (i.e. narrower) in the in-the-money series and more exaggerated (i.e. wider) in the out-of-the-money series, particularly for a high beta stock. This is, once again, largely a function of gearing. While the most crucial decision concerning the choice of expiry date will inevitably be determined by an investment judgement on the likely course of the share price, the time value differential within an option class over the three expiry periods is an important element in the final selection.

Again, there can be no hard-and-fast rules for the choice of expiry date: each case must be reviewed in isolation and adjudicated according to its own particular investment merits. Nevertheless, it has to be said that, in general terms, the three-month time scale is often the most attractive to write for two main reasons.

(1) On the assumption that the underlying share price remains unchanged throughout the full life of an option, the latter will lose something in the region of 50% of its time value over the first six months or so. Time values waste away most rapidly in the final three months before expiry. Armed with this knowledge, the option writer wishing to capitalise on fast-decreasing time values must sell the short three-month options. He must also be mindful of the fact that the out-of-the-money series (particularly in high volatility stocks) will tend to maintain a high time value almost right up to the expiry date. In the example of LSI, it would not have been surprising to find the July 330 series trading at around six points up to within a week or two of expiry, even if the share price had never achieved the strike price from day one. Thus, while writing out-of-the-money series may be considered 'safer' than an at-the-money call (from the viewpoint of minimising the risk of losing the stock), the writer will invariably have to wait almost until expiry date itself before he recoups the full premium from the sale as it eventually wastes to zero.

(2) Theoretically at least, the annualised return from a *three*-month call option will be considerably more attractive to a writer than the comparable figure (over 12 months) for either a six- or nine-month option. Of course, it is far too simplistic to assume that the movement of the underlying stock will conveniently permit a factor of four being applied to the three-month rate or a factor of two to the six-month rate, etc. Nevertheless, it is more than reasonable to assume that the time valuation for three months taken over three consecutive periods will exceed the initial rate quoted for the nine-month call. The main reason for this is not too sophisticated: it is largely a function of the predominantly heavier volume that is always a feature of the short three-month expiry date, whether for buyers or writers.

Simultaneous purchase of stock and choice of expiry period

Many private investors feel that the volatility of modern stock markets is so immense that it is too difficult even to attempt to read future price movements over a given time scale. On the important assumption that the investor is content to hold a particular share on its fundamental investment merits, the traded options market offers the prospect of eminently reasonable returns on capital employed via a purchase of the underlying security and the simultaneous execution of a written option against it. (The collateral rules allow this to be achieved by paying for the stock immediately rather than waiting until account day, thus providing cash cover until the stock is settled.)

The investor adopting this conservative strategy is paying little regard to market timing other than in his selection of an expiry date and strike price, the combination of which will produce a series to meet his minimum requirements in terms of return on capital employed. In early May 1980 the aspiring covered writer, content to purchase any or all of the underlying portfolios of stocks, would have considered which option series to write. [May 1980 is a good time to choose for this example since the market (Financial Times Index) had dropped 14% over the preceding months and premium levels were hardly exotic.] The choice of exercise price would be determined largely by the expenses involved in taking up the underlying security – an out-of-the money series had to be selected to allow a reasonable profit after all expenses if the share price rose and the stock was sold through assignment of the option. The only real decision therefore rested with the choice of expiry date, i.e. the July or October series. The relevant figures are given in Table 6.2 (allowance has been made for full expenses throughout the exercise); on a unit of 10,000 shares and 10 contracts, the returns in columns 5 and 6 (left to right) are *net* calculations.

If no action is taken from purchase of the stock and the writing of the call to expiry of the option, only one of two permutations can happen.

(1) If the share price rises above the strike price, resulting in the option being exercised against the writer, he will be obliged to deliver his shares at the strike price. His profit on the transaction will be the difference between the purchase price of the shares and the sum of the exercise price plus the option premium. The GEC example via the July 390 series would work out as follows:

Purchase 376   Sell 390 + 18 = 408   Profit = 32

The fifth column in Table 6.2 expresses this profit as a percentage of the purchase price of the shares, allowing for all

Table 6.2

Stock	Offer price of stock (p)	Option series	Option bid price (p)	% appreciation if stock called	% book cost write down if option abandoned
July expiry					
GMH	128	Jul. 130	8	3.6	5.8
GEC	376	Jul. 390	18	5.0	4.5
BP	338	Jul. 360	18	8.2	5.0
ICI	376	Jul. 390	17	4.8	4.2
CUA	135	Jul. 140	7	4.8	4.7
October expiry					
GMH	128	Oct. 130	11½	6.1	8.3
GEC	376	Oct. 390	34	9.0	8.5
BP	338	Oct. 360	30	11.5	8.3
ICI	376	Oct. 390	22	6.0	5.5
CUA	135	Oct. 140	13	9.0	9.0

expenses. In this instance a gain of 5% was achieved over three months.

(2) If the share price does not achieve the strike price within the life of the option, the latter will eventually expire worthless and the writer will pocket the premium. The sixth column expresses that premium gain as a percentage of the purchase price of the share, again after all expenses. In the same GEC example the premium receipts (18 points) were 4.5% (over three months), enabling book cost to be written down by that amount (less capital gains tax).

The figures show quite clearly that these 'rates' of return are more than acceptable, given the neutral investment timing stance adopted by the investor. Of course, if the share price moved up substantially, a high-opportunity cost loss would be suffered, while if the shares dropped dramatically the option proceeds would give a very limited protection on the downside. Nevertheless, use of this conservative written option strategy in these circumstances is certainly preferable to simply buying the shares straight and keeping fingers crossed. It is surprising how many investors do just this whether consciously or otherwise!

Our conservative investor in the GEC example initially took a neutral view of the share when he wrote the July 390 series at 18. He was mindful of the fact that the company was due to report its final trading figures and dividend before the expiry day of his option, but he was sympathetic to the innumerable bearish analytical forecasts emanating from the City. On 3 July GEC announced a package of results that took the market by surprise, sending the share price up dramatically and the bears scurrying to cover their positions. Our investor was sufficiently impressed by this performance from the company that he regretted the imminent loss of his shares through his written option. He was still bullish for the share price despite the short-term mark-up. Is there anything he could do to extricate himself from his present position and accommodate his new investment criteria? The answer is yes: he could 'walk up' the option.

Walking up an option

As we have seen, our GEC option writer aims to participate in the increase in the price of the underlying share. His attitude is now more positive and more aggressive: he is willing to forgo a portion of his protection against a possible decline in the share price. Thus, as the price of the stock increases, he buys in a previously written option (i.e. July 390) and writes a new option with a higher exercise price and/or more distant maturity, in order to establish a higher sales price should the stock be called away from him. I will pursue the arithmetic of the current example (expenses have been ignored).

Initial position: Purchased stock at 376. Wrote July 390 at 18.
By the account in which the July series were to expire the situation had been transformed:

	July 390	*October 500*
Share price (p)	*offer price (p)*	*bid price (p)*
489	98	27

STAGE 1
Strategy: Walk up the option – from July 390 to October 500.
Implementation: Buy back (closing) the July 390 at 98, and write (opening) the Oct. 500 at 27.
Profit/loss (−) on transaction to date:

Stock	*Options*
+ 113 (376 to 489)	− 80 (98 less 18)

New position: Assuming exercise of the option, a sale price of 527 has been achieved.

STAGE 2
By the account in which the October series were to expire the situation was as follows:

	October 500	*January 500*	*January 550*
Share price (p)	*offer price (p)*	*bid price (p)*	*bid price (p)*
515	20	50	25

Strategy: Still bullish – walk up October 500 to January 500 or January 550.
Implementation: Buy back (closing) the October 500 at 20, and write (opening) the January 500 at 50 or January 550 at 25.
Profit/loss (−) on transaction to date:

	Stock	*Options*
	+ 139 (376 to 515)	− 73 (80 less 7)

New position: Assuming exercise of the option, a sale price of 550 or 575.

The investor has thus achieved his desired objective, i.e. to increase his total return (exercise price plus net premium) if the shares are eventually called from him.

Walking down an option

As the name suggests, 'walking down' an option is the converse of 'walking up' in every sense. It is a strategy suitable for a declining market (rather than a rising market), particularly where the decline is persistent and extends over a reasonable time scale. It is *not* the vehicle for attempting to capitalise (in highly volatile markets) on a sharp, short-term, technical retracement in a share price. The object of the exercise is to protect the value of a portfolio against a decline in share prices where the decision not to sell the underlying security has been taken. Increased downside protection is thus given full weighting in a strategy that accepts a higher opportunity cost if the shares rise rather than fall. To achieve this protection it is imperative to write at- or in-the-money series with full time values: as the share price drops, the existing written position is closed (by buying it back) and walked down to the next lower exercise price. Protection of capital is thus the overriding consideration in this strategy.

I have suggested that 'walking down' is suitable only in circumstances where a considerable percentage fall in the underlying share price is envisaged over a reasonable time scale. If this strategy is implemented in an attempt to capitalise on short-term market swings in high beta stocks, the whiplash effect of stock/option movements allied to relatively high dealing costs will, in all probability, prove psychologically demoralising and financially crippling. You have been warned!

Writing out-of-the-money series – a very conservative strategy

Earlier in this chapter I referred to the large number of investors whose major risk in writing options is associated with loss or potential loss of the underlying security. This emanates primarily from (a) fear of missing a rise in equities from an already high liquidity base, and thus compounding the felony by losing existing stock through the exercise of written option positions, and (b) the desire to avoid the exposure of a large capital profit liable to a substantial tax charge. Hopefully, I have demonstrated how these fears can be largely nullified by buying back the written option and walking up the series. Nevertheless, the psychological impact of these fears is a sufficient deterrent to some investors, and has to be recognised, accepted and accommodated.

It was my opinion, when the Traded Options Market opened in 1978, that it was eminently possible to effect a highly conservative strategy founded on writing out-of-the-money calls against cover of the underlying security, which would provide a low risk factor of having this security called: the seller will thus write options (the vast majority of which will subsequently waste to zero) and pocket the premiums. It was my belief that the level of these premiums should *comfortably exceed* the gross dividend income from the underlying stock over any twelve-month period. Practical experience of putting this theory into practice over the past three years has simply confirmed and re-inforced the earlier judgements. A little later I will review and analyse how the strategy was achieved (or not) each year up to the time of writing, and how it can be implemented *consistently* in the future. The figures really are quite startling! Before we consider these results, it is necessary to define the game-plan and the operational rules governing it.

The immense volatility of modern stock market movements (as we have seen) is such that there may be one or possibly two major opportunities each year to write options which subsequently expire worthless. Of course, there will be many more opportunities within any twelve-month period for the aggressive trader to write options successfully. For the purposes of this exercise, however, we are concerned primarily with highlighting the one or two opportunities which may occur each year, providing the over-bought conditions against which options can be written *almost* across the board – almost but (obviously) not entirely. Common sense (apart from any technical expertise) will sometimes temper the inclusion of a particular stock in the general recommendation. While the gold boom was in full flow in 1980, the risks of writing even heavy out-of-the-money options in Consolidated Goldfields clearly outweighed the maximum reward of a relatively small option premium.

Institutional fund managers and many private investors participating in the option market for the first time will require a strategy for writing covered calls which is essentially highly conservative and relatively straightforward, and one which avoids the necessity for constant monitoring of the share/option price for fear of losing the stock through exercise of the option. Writing heavy out-of-the-money options for a respectable premium when the market is technically over-bought remains the simplest and most effective way of achieving the aims of this exercise with the minimum of administrative and managerial aggravation. I adhered largely to this principle over the past three years to achieve the results analysed later in the text.

Regrettably, I do not have the space here to give a detailed consideration of over-bought market conditions: while it remains a fascinating and intriguing subject, it is also a complex one which should not be treated too casually. Suffice it to say that, while the numerous OB/OS indicators published regularly in the financial columns will obviously differ by degree of interpretation, the one ingredient common to all over-bought signals is a steep percentage rise over a relatively short time scale. The February–May 1979 'Thatcher' bull market, the sharp movements in January–February and May–July 1980 are perfectly good examples of rises which went too far too quickly and gave birth to temporarily over-bought conditions. This, in turn, produced an expansion in the option premiums as the momentum of the herd instinct built up to a crescendo. This is usually an excellent time to start to look for attractive out-of-the-money writing opportunities. In a publication in 1978 I suggested (with tongue in cheek) that we may have found a partial solution to the problem of stock market timing. *Chamberlain's law* for a major commitment to covered option writing read: 'when the investment community consensus is unreservedly bullish, liquidity high, equity bargains rising, option volume at record levels, unit trust sales breaking new records, write out-of-the-money options.'

This is possibly too cynical, but the suggested action would have avoided the pitfalls associated with virtually every bull move in the FT Index over the 500 level during the past decade and it is, after all, just another way of presenting the creed of the successful professional trader 'buy when it's flat and sell when it's good' or 'when the ducks quack, feed them': one can afford not to be stingy with the fodder in these circumstances! Of course, the more protracted the fall in share prices, the sharper the eventual rise will be, as the 1973–75 bear market revealed quite dramatically. However, the risks of writing out-of-the-money options too early once in a while will be more than made good over the years.

I must warn, however, that a haphazard or undisciplined approach to such an option writing programme will not produce the desired

Table 6.3

Stock	Date	Stock price (p)	Recommended action	Option proceeds	Time scale (weeks)	Stock price at option expiry (p)	Annual gross dividend paid	Total option proceeds taken
Calendar year 1978								
CTD	25 May	127	Sell Jul. 130	6	10	120		
	21 July	119	Sell Oct. 130	7	13	119	11.2	13.0
M & S	14 Aug.	87	Sell Oct. 90	5	9	84		
	23 Oct.	87	Sell Jan. 90	6	13	84	3.6*	11.0
							*Adjusted for scrip issue.	
GMH	30 Oct.	108	Sell Jan. 120	7	11	112	6.6	7.0
BP	2 Oct.	895	Sell Jan. 950	35	16	886	34.5	35.0
GEC	5 June	261	Sell Jul. 280	6	6	264		
	11 Dec.	337	Sell Jan. 360	7	7	317	6.4	13.0
Calendar year 1979								
CTD	21 Jan.	117	Sell Apr. 120	6.5	13	102		
	30 April	112	Sell Jul. 120	6.5	12	83	12.2	13.0
M & S	30 April	126	Sell Jul. 130	12	12	112		
	1 Oct.	104	Sell Jan. 110	6	16	90	4.2	18.0

Company	Date							
GMH	23 April	171	Sell Jul. 180	13.5	13	141*	8.0	13.5
BP	14 May	1,108	Sell Jul. 1,300	54	9	1,210	67.6	86.0*
	10 Dec.	364	Sell Jan. 400	8	7	342		
GEC	30 April	437	Sell Jul. 460	26	13	358	10.0	39.0
	3 Sept.	383	Sell Oct. 390	13	6	365		
Calendar year 1980								
CTD	10 March	70	Sell Apr. 70	4.5	6	66	12.2	9.5
	24 Nov.	68	Sell Jan. 70	5	8	54		
M & S	25 Feb.	90	Sell Apr. 100	4	8	88	4.8	10.0
	1 Dec.	116	Sell Jan. 120	6	7	115		
GMH	25 Feb.	131	Sell Apr. 140	4.5	8	125	9.7	9.5
	16 Sept.	157	Sell Oct. 160	5	4	156		
BP	25 Feb.	391	Sell Apr. 440	9	8	334	26.1	31.0
	1 Dec.	480	Sell Jan. 500	22	7	394		
GEC	25 Feb.	375	Sell Apr. 420	8	8	375	12.5	31.0
	1 Dec.	613	Sell Jan. 650	23	7	587		

*Ex rights.

*Adjusted for scrip issue.

result and could prove an expensive exercise in more ways than one. The history of the mid-1970s provides ample evidence of the immense volatility of price movement which has become a feature of modern stock markets. I can see little evidence that this volatility will moderate to any significant degree over the next decade; indeed, it could get worse. In such circumstances, writing the wrong option at the wrong time can be disastrous, as some early participants have found. The generally unexpected early-January (1980) equity rally took the FT Index up 48 points in eleven trading days: Marks & Spencer rose from 75 to 93 over this period. An investor who had written the January 70 options against his holding was faced with the probable loss of his shares at the wrong price via an option that had risen from 8 to 24. Should he buy his option back at a substantial loss, simply to avoid losing his underlying stock, and end up out of the stock altogether? Should he buy more shares in the market to cover his likely liability to deliver his stock through exercise of the option? Or should he do nothing other than cross everything and hope that the price of the stock/options falls back? An unenviable problem indeed, but not an uncommon one for the uninitiated (in the capacity of either client or sponsor). You have been warned! Avoid writing options, even the heavy out-of-the-money series when the market in general or a stock in particular is heavily over-sold. Do not write options in these circumstances, no matter how expensive and technically attractive the option appears. For the purposes of this exercise, the main objective is to avoid loss of the underlying stock through assignment (the cost of replacement is expensive and eats into the profitability of the strategy quite dramatically). Writing options haphazardly increases the risks of this happening: avoid it whenever possible.

We can now consider the results of implementing this strategy, up to the time of writing since inception of the market in 1978. The prime tasks are, firstly, to secure option premiums through written options which comfortably exceed the dividend income from the underlying stock over any twelve-month period, and secondly, in so doing, to attempt to avoid loss of the underlying stock wherever possible. Five of the original ten stocks introduced in April 1978 were selected for this exercise and heavy weighting was given to high beta stocks to make the task as difficult as possible. Table 6.3 shows the results over the period from April 1978 to January 1981 expiry: the dates refer to when action on the writing side was taken, and the last two columns (on the right) compare directly the annual gross dividend paid on the underlying security and the total option proceeds secured over the same period.

The following analysis and observations can be made from Table 6.3.

(1) During 1978 the declared strategy enabled the target to be achieved, producing satisfactory results from CTD, GMH and BP and excellent figures for M & S and GEC. The results of implementing the policy in 1979 were even better across the board. 1980 proved to be a slightly more difficult year and I failed to achieve the target for CTD and marginally missed the one for GMH; BP was also a bit of a struggle. It is interesting and somewhat ironic to observe that, in CTD's case, the performance of the share price was so poor in 1980 that the premium levels were paltry and unexciting for much of the year, while, in BP's case, the strength of the share price early in the year and again during the late summer created difficulties in the timing of option sales to ensure worthless premiums at expiry without risking loss of the underlying stock. In late November/ early December I concluded that the market was sufficiently over-bought to warrant sales of the heavy out-of-the-money series in M & S, BP and GEC: the corresponding premiums in the cases of CTD and GMH were far too unattractive to write at that time (due to an uninspiring share price performance). For holders of CTD the risk of writing a marginally out-of-the-money series (i.e. Jan. 70s) was considered a reasonable one; in the case of GMH (with figures due early in January) the risks were considered too high and hence no action was taken.

(2) In no case over three years to date was the underlying security called: thus dividend income was maintained. The benefits of this strategy are highlighted in the case of a high-multiple, low-dividend-return company like GEC, where the holder of the underlying security has enjoyed a most exciting and profitable ride since 1978. The successful covered writer has enjoyed the same capital appreciation on his investment in the stock. Additionally, he has achieved a substantial 'extra' return in the form of expired option proceeds (taxed at the appropriate capital gains tax rate).

(3) In the main, I deliberately chose (to write) the heaviest out-of-the-money option series to ensure and re-iterate the excessive conservatism of the strategy. There were innumerable occasions over the period under review when it would have been possible to make the results of the exercise look even more startling by writing series only marginally out-of-the-money or even at-the-

93

money. However, I resisted the temptation in an endeavour to show how consistently the strategy could be achieved.

(4) No allowance has been made for the investment 'use' of the written proceeds received: premiums received from writing calls covered by the underlying security are credited or paid out the following day. This additional cash flow can be significant in any calculation of total return on capital employed, whether it is placed on deposit earning interest or re-invested in additional shares upon which further options can be written.

How can any sensible investor ignore option writing along these lines?

Before I move on to review some of the more aggressive option writing strategies, I believe that this is a suitable juncture to pause to consider the extensive range of cover and margin permissible under the rules of the Stock Exchange for prospective covered writers.

Cover and margin requirements for covered writers

All bargains in traded options will be transacted for 'cash' settlement. Every writer of a traded option contract in an 'opening selling transaction', who will have been credited with the premiums due to him, must deposit the appropriate cover or margin with LOCH (London Option Clearing House) before 10.00 a.m. on the following business day.

(1) Cover

Cover is defined as the deposit with LOCH of a confirmation by an approved bank either that it holds the underlying security for the written contract in the name of its nominee company to the order of LOCH or that the underlying security is in course of registration into the name of its nominee company and will, when registered, be held to the order of LOCH. Investors intending to act as covered writers should make contact with a broker specialising in the traded option market as soon as possible in order that he may make the necessary arrangements to comply with this regulation.

(2) Alternative cover

Convertible issues, bearer shares, Euro-dollar convertible bonds and American depository receipts, whose equity is also a traded option class, may be used as cover for written option contracts, subject to the conditions set out below.

Convertible issues:

Imperial Group Limited: 8% convertible unsecured loan stock 1985/90; £2,000 of this stock will be acceptable cover for one Imperial Group contract of 1,000 shares.

Land Securities Investment Trust Limited:

  (i) 5⅞% convertible unsecured loan stock 1983; £1,500 of this stock will be acceptable cover for one LSI contract of 1,000 shares.

 (ii) 6¼% convertible unsecured loan stock 1985; £2,000 of this stock will be acceptable cover for one LSI contract of 1,000 shares.

(iii) 10% convertible unsecured loan stock 1990/5; £2,000 of this stock will be acceptable cover for one LSI contract of 1,000 shares.

Investors wishing to deposit convertible stock as cover may do so only in multiples of the amounts shown. A number of contracts in the same class may be covered by a combination of equity and convertible submitted in 'whole lots'. However, under no circumstances will mixed margin (i.e. cash plus equity/convertible) for a single contract be permitted.

Bearer shares:

Shell Transport & Trading Company Limited bearer 25p ordinary shares, Rio Tinto Zinc Corporation Limited bearer 25p ordinary shares and Rio Tinto Zinc Corporation accumulator shares are acceptable cover for written positions in their corresponding classes.

Euro-dollar convertible bonds:

ICI International Finance Limited: 6¾% convertible guaranteed bonds 1997; 10 convertible guaranteed bonds will be acceptable as cover for one ICI contract of 1,000 shares.

The conditions governing the use of these are as follows.

  (i) Euro-dollar convertible bonds used as cover must be held in either Euroclear or Cedel and accompanied by a signed undertaking from the client or broker (as appropriate) stating that:
     (a) in the case of bonds held in Euroclear: that the bonds are being held to the order of Barclays Bank Limited, Angel Court, London EC2;
     (b) in the case of bonds held in Cedel: that the bonds are being

95

held to the order of Barclays Bank International Limited, Old Broad Street, London EC2.

(ii) Mixed 'margin' (i.e. cash plus equity/convertible) for a single contract will not be permitted.

(iii) A number of contracts in the same class may be covered by a combination of equity and convertible submitted in 'whole lots'.

(iv) Euro-dollar bonds pledged as cover will incur charges by Barclays Bank Limited or Barclays Bank International Limited (as appropriate). Such charges are to be borne by the writer.

American depository receipts:

ADRs issued in respect of shares of companies whose equity is also a traded option class may be used as cover for written option contracts in that class.

The conditions governing the use of ADRs are as follows.

(i) ADRs used as cover must be deposited with Barclays Bank International Limited, New York, (BBI) and accompanied by Pledge Form 2 stating that such ADRs are being held to the order of the London Option Clearing House.

(ii) Assignments issued in respect of option contracts covered by the deposit of ADRs are to be satisfied by delivery of London registered stock on London terms (ex dividend, ex rights, etc.) unless otherwise agreed by both exerciser and assignee.

(iii) ADRs pledged as cover will incur charges by BBI of US $25 on deposit and a further charge of US $25 on release from pledge. Such charges are to be borne by the writer.

(3) *Margin*

The writer of a traded option contract who does not wish to deposit with LOCH the cover of the underlying security may deposit, as margin, a cash sum equivalent to 25% of the value of the underlying security, adjusted by the amount by which the option series stands in- or out-of-the-money. The sum is subject to daily adjustment to conform with the movements in the market price of the underlying security. I will return to this subject in greater detail under the heading of 'uncovered option writing'.

(4) *Alternative margin*

Treasury bills:

These may be lodged as margin for open written contracts. The value of the Treasury bill is calculated as the face value of the bill, less 2.5% or such other figure as the Council may notify member firms.

'Gilts':

British funds, registered at the Bank of England, may be used as alternative margin on the terms stipulated below.

(i) The value of British funds pledged will be calculated by reference to a price list published regularly by LOCH and in the case of:

   (a) funds not having more than 5 years to final redemption will be reduced by 5% of that value or to par, whichever is the lower;

   (b) funds having more than 5 years to final redemption will be reduced by 10% of that value or to par, whichever is the lower;

   (c) partly paid stock will be reduced by 10% of the fully paid value of the stock in registered form or to par, whichever is the lower. Partly paid stock lodged as margin will require replacement by cash margin or full cover two days before due payment date or any further or final call.

(ii) The initial deposit and any subsequent deposit of British funds pledged in respect of an option contract(s) shall be accepted as alternative margin only if delivery is made in amounts of £1,000 nominal or more.

(iii) Dividend payment on British funds pledged. Non-resident clients having British funds pledged at the custodian bank will receive dividend payments net of tax and will be required to make their own arrangements for reclaiming tax deducted at source.

(iv) Partly paid British funds as margin. Where partly paid British funds are deposited with an authorised bank as margin, and arrangements are made between that bank and a broker or clearing member for the bank to pay a call on their behalf, then, provided such stock remains pledged to the order of LOCH and under the bank's control, it may continue to be used as margin during the period of payment of the call.

PARTIALLY COVERED OPTION WRITING

Known in America as 'variable hedging' or 'ratio writing', this variation involves writing one option covered by the underlying shares and one or more options which are uncovered. The aims of this strategy are identical to those of the fully covered option writer: the difference simply reflects the magnitude of the additional risk involved in seeking additional or extra premium income, increased cash flow and increased protection against a possible price decline.

The investor, recognising a temporary, 'over-bought' market, may be disinclined to sell any of his underlying share portfolio, fearing that the downward movement may be insufficient to warrant the expense of selling and repurchasing at a later date. He may, however, seek some protection against his anticipated decline, the extent of which he cannot predict accurately in advance. Ratio writing can provide such a 'hedge'.

The strategy involves writing two, three or more calls: the more calls written, the greater the scope for the underlying shares to fall before the position incurs a net loss, i.e. when the cost difference exceeds the totality of premium income. The ratio of uncovered options written to the cover of the underlying shares will be a function strictly of the investor's assessment of downside potential and the extent of his risk preferences. The hedge writer thus establishes a price band within the parameters of which he remains in profit over the life of the option: obviously, the closer the underlying shares hug the exercise price, the greater the eventual profit to the writer. By the same token, the higher the ratio of uncovered calls written, the greater the risk exposure should the share move out of the protection of the upper parameter of the price band. Let us consider some examples, using IMP options to illustrate these points.

Assume: (1) that the investor owns 1,000 shares in IMP;
(2) that he writes IMP Feb. 80 calls as a protection against an anticipated fall in the share price.

(a) Options written with the shares standing at 80 (at-the-money)

Write two Feb. 80 calls at 8 premium
Total premium income (TPI)   16
Downside protection to   64   (80 − 16)
Upside protection only to   96   (80 + 16)

The profit band is thus 64 − 96, i.e. 32 points, and the investor has bought protection against a 20% fall in IMP shares.

(b) Options written with the shares standing at 76 (out-of-the-money)

Write two Feb. 80 calls at 5 premium
TPI   10

Downside protection to   66   (76 − 10)
Upside protection only to   94   (14 + 80)

$$\left(= \frac{\text{Premium} + \text{Difference between share price \& exercise price (EP)}}{\text{Number of uncovered options}} + \text{EP} \right)$$

The profit band is thus 66 – 94, i.e. 28 points, and offers protection against a 13% fall in IMP shares.

(c) Options written with the shares at 83 (in-the-money)

    Write two Feb. 70 calls at 15 premium
    TPI   30
    Downside protection to   53   (83 − 30)
    Upside protection only to   87   (17 + 70)

$$\left(= \frac{\text{Premium} - \text{Difference between share price \& exercise price (EP)}}{\text{Number of uncovered options}} + \text{EP} \right)$$

The profit band is thus 53 − 87, i.e. 34 points, and offers protection against a 36% fall in IMP shares. This is the most bearish variation of the three, offering the heaviest protection from a sizeable fall in the share price but only marginal upside protection.

A modification of this strategy might involve writing one option against the cover of the underlying shares and subsequently writing further options at lower exercise prices. Such a ploy might suit the investor anticipating falling prices but who wishes to witness the actuality of some price weakness before making total commitment to the strategy.

(d) 1,000 IMP shares valued at 80

    Write one Feb. 80 call at 8 premium
    One month later the shares have slumped to 72
    Write one Feb. 70 call at 6 premium
    TPI   14
    Downside protection to   66   (80 − 14)
    Upside protection only to   82   (70 + 12)

The profit band is thus 66 − 82, i.e. 16 points, offering protection against a 17.5% fall in the shares. Obviously, this somewhat cautious approach offers less downside protection than some of the earlier models reflecting more positive, adventurous attitudes. Additional protection can be achieved simply by writing more uncovered calls (see below).

(e) 1,000 shares in IMP valued at 80

Write three Feb. 80 calls at 7 premium
TPI   21
Downside protection to   59   (80 − 21)
Upside protection only to   90.5 (80 + 10.5)

The profit band is thus 59 – 90.5, i.e. 31.5 points, offering protection against a 26% fall in the shares. It must never be forgotten that the greater the ratio of uncovered calls written, the larger the exposure if the shares move outside the upper parameters of the price band: it can be a recipe for financial disaster if used irresponsibly or too casually.

The 'variable hedger', anticipating higher than lower prices, will simply reverse the procedures outlined earlier. He would write either out-of-the-money options or a combination of at-the-money and out-of-the-money calls. He may walk up the option by buying in low strike price calls and writing higher strike calls. His degree of optimism and his risk acceptance will dictate the ratio of uncovered calls written.

Variable hedging offers an almost endless number of permutations, limited only by the imagination of the writer. Being aware of his profit parameters at the outset, the investor has ample scope for manoeuvre, and is thus able to monitor and control any future action on a day-by-day basis. As his expectations and assessment change, so will his strategy.

Margin/collateral requirements

The collateral rules for a covered writer will apply to that part of the 'hedge' covered by the underlying security. Margin requirements for the uncovered writer (dealt with in detail in the next section) will apply to all uncovered contracts written.

UNCOVERED OPTION WRITING

The writer of calls without the cover of the underlying shares is 'going short' of the shares in question (i.e. selling a bear). Technically, his exposure on the upside is unlimited, insulated only by the premium receipts less expenses. However, the Option Exchange enables the 'naked' writer to limit his liability and control his potential loss in normal market conditions through the facility of buying back the call at any time. Also, the provision of a price limit system, if used intelligently, can limit the risk exposure on the upside. It cannot, however,

provide protection against a sharp, substantial price adjustment resulting from a surprise take-over bid or similar price-sensitive news.

The basic objectives of the 'naked' writer are similar to those of the
covered writer discussed earlier. The variance in the techniques utilised
will reflect simply the differing risk preferences. More often than not,
the temperament of the 'naked' writer will dictate a more positive
attitude to his assessment of any particular trend of price movement,
and subsequently a more aggressive approach in the attempt to capitalise upon it. For both, the maximum profit will be the premium receipts
less expenses. However, the uncovered writer hopes not to commit
capital to the purchase of the underlying shares and hence to improve
substantially his overall return on capital employed. He will be required, however, to deposit a minimum sum equivalent to 25%* of the
value of the underlying security, adjusted by the amount by which the
option series stands in- or out-of-the-money. This is calculated daily,
based upon the 3.30 p.m. closing price of the underlying security.

Example
   (1) IMP shares stand at 72 in the market.
   (2) *Calls available* (3 months)   *Premiums*
          IMP Feb. 70   5¾
          IMP Feb. 80   1½
   (3) For statistical ease, ignore expenses.

(A) *Margin requirement of uncovered writer of IMP 70 call*

25% of the underlying security price	18p per share
Plus Amount by which the option is	
in-the-money (72 − 70)	2p per share
	20p per share

(B) *Margin requirement of uncovered writer of IMP 80 call*

25% of the underlying security price	18p per share
Less Amount by which the option is	
out-of-the-money (80 − 72)	8p per share
	10p per share

Margin will thus be calculated at 25% of the underlying share price
plus or minus in- or out-of-the-money: this figure is considered adequate
protection overall against the risk of an upward movement in the price of

---

*Individual firms of stockbrokers may require a figure in excess of this minimum level
recommended and required under the rules of the Stock Exchange.

the underlying security during the ensuing business day. The writer's liability is obviously increased to the extent that the option is in-the-money, and likewise reduced if the option is out-of-the-money. Table 6.4 compares, over the minimum three-month period of the option, the return achieved on the cash margin required for the uncovered position compared with its covered counterpart.

Table 6.4

Writer's position	Cash/collateral required per share	Three-months' return (PRM received as % of cash committed)	Annualised return
(1) Uncovered writer of 70 call	20	28.75	115.00
(2) Uncovered writer of 80 call	10	15.00	60.00
(3) Covered writer of 70 call	72	7.98	31.92
(4) Covered writer of 80 call	72	2.08	8.32

The figures relating to positions (1) and (2) give some idea of the quarterly and annual returns that the uncovered writer is able to achieve on a low cash margin investment. Indeed, it is precisely this premium return, expressed as a percentage of the cash margin re-quired, that highlights the relative attractions of successful uncovered writing when compared with the alternative covered position. These figures also tend to understate the potential return, to the extent that they assume that the written position is taken at the very beginning of each quarter and make no allowance for the re-investment of the original money sum and/or the premium receipts accumulated over the four quarters. On the other hand, positions (1) and (2) *overstate* the potential return by assuming that the price of the underlying stock does not move up over the life of the option (thus necessitating more cash margin), which is rarely the case. (By the same token, however, if the shares continue to fall, less cash margin is required and the return improves proportionately.)

Commissions have been ignored in this exercise and the assumption has been made that all the options expire worthless, i.e. remain un-exercised. In practice, of course, many of them will be exercised against, resulting in losses to the writer and thus considerably reducing profitability. Nevertheless, high percentage profits of this magnitude may be achieved by the shrewd, uncovered writer who is capable of reading market trends successfully.

While a low margin requirement makes the achievement of high profit returns possible, the daily adjustment of margins can render the

writing of heavily out-of-the-money calls an expensive exercise, i.e.
tying up too much capital for a poor effective return. The illustration in
Table 6.5 will clarify the point; the position of the uncovered writer of
the 80 call (see Table 6.4) has been taken. As can be seen in Table 6.5,
a rise in the market price of the underlying security of 5.5% causes a
50% leap in the margin requirements and consequent worsening of the
percentage return.

Table 6.5

Exercise price	80
Market price	72
Margin requirement 25% of 72	18
Less Difference between market	
price and exercise price	8
Real margin	10
Premium	1½
Return	15%
If the shares rise 4:	
Exercise price	80
Market price	76
Margin required	19
Less Difference between market	
price and exercise price	4
Real margin	15
Return	10%

It is worth repeating at this juncture that the uncovered writer can be
called upon at any time to purchase the underlying shares at the then-
prevailing market price in order to deliver them to the exerciser at the
exercise price. He has no control over this contingency other than in the
initial selection of the particular calls written: his choice will obviously
be affected by this important consideration. While the historic evidence
of trading options both in America and in this country to date reveals
that the likelihood of exercise against a writer, whether covered or
otherwise, until well into the life of the option is remote, nevertheless
the uncovered writer in particular *must not* take it for granted.

From the discussion so far it should be clear that writing uncovered
calls should be attempted only by those investors fully cognisant of the

substantial risks involved and financially able to assume them. However, it should not necessarily be assumed that this area of the options medium automatically excludes anyone but the market professionals – correct assessment of market movements is by no means solely the preserve of stockbrokers and investment advisors! It does, however, assume a clinical, unemotional attitude to market trends on the part of the writer, coupled with an almost ruthless ability to change tack unequivocally if an earlier decision looks wrong. Constant attention to price changes, whether by the option writer, his stockbroker, or both, is mandatory.

In the main, investors would be well advised to attempt the strategy of uncovered writing *only* to accommodate an investment view that is *very positively* bearish of either an individual stock or, preferably, of the market as a whole. If the market is considered heavily over-bought and ripe for a significant setback, then by all means give uncovered writing a go. If the investment case does not match up to these criteria, leave uncovered option writing well alone – the risks of open-ended liability clearly outweigh the maximum benefits. I will return to this in detail later.

My view of the London market at the end of April 1979 was that a 100-point rise in the FT Index from mid-February had left it extremely over-bought, even before the final celebratory excesses of an 'inevitable' Tory election victory were given expression. I was positive that the market was ripe for a significant setback, despite the fact that the bulls were rampant, since many projected a rise to over 600 in the Index within weeks of the Thatcher dream becoming a reality. Through the option market it was already possible to discount that 'assured' level of the Index by writing the three-month out-of-the-money calls. Table 6.6 reviews the arithmetic relating to five stocks available at the end of April. The final column shows the relative levels by which the then-prevailing share prices could be forward sold, on the assumption that the options were exercised against the writer: the range was 6.6% to 12.9% (of the share price). Writing the relevant options to accommodate a positively bearish, but not an aggressively bearish, view of the market seemed an eminently reasonable strategy. An investor wishing to adopt the more aggressive stance (i.e. one who was totally convinced that the market would fall) would have written the in-the-money option series (shown in brackets); the considerably higher premium levels reveal quite clearly the scope for increased profitability. (They also offer considerably less upside protection if the view subsequently turns out to be totally wrong.)

Table 6.6

Stock	Stock price (p)	July options	Option bid price (p)	Effective sale price of stock	% difference between current price and effective sale price
BP	1,237	1,300 (1,200)	50 (125)	1,350 (1,325)	9.1 (7.1)
GMH	173	180 (160)	12 (23)	192 (183)	11.0 (5.7)
M & S	124	130 (120)	9 (13)	139 (133)	12.1 (7.3)
GEC	429	460 (420)	22 (43)	482 (463)	12.4 (7.9)
CTD	112	120 (110)	6 (9)	126 (119)	12.5 (6.3)

As the history books now relate, the victorious Conservative bull market lasted just one hour into the following business day once the result had been confirmed: from then on, stock prices went into free fall. All these option series expired worthless at the end of July, with the exception of the BP July 1,200 series, which had an intrinsic value of 35. It would thus have been bought back at that level for a gross profit of 90 (125 − 35) per written contract. At the very worst (and only for a short period of time) the uncovered writer would have been asked for a cash deposit of 225 per contract, allowing for the credit of the 125 premium written – not a bad return on capital employed over three months!

Thus, the return on capital employed from a naked writing option scheme can be most appetising if the writer reads the market correctly. I could list numerous examples over the past three years (up to the time of writing) where this strategy has reaped handsome rewards. I could list even more examples over the same time scale where an unsuccess-ful uncovered written position could have spelt financial disaster. I do not wish to sound too dramatic; nor do I have the desire to frighten investors from ever using this strategy. However, I consider that it would be irresponsible to leave readers under any illusions as to the immense dangers involved in too casual or undisciplined an approach to this facet of option writing. Accordingly, I will risk the criticism of being too negative in my approach to the subject by highlighting three examples of potential financial 'wipe-out', all of which emanated from a decision at the outset which looked neither irresponsible nor statisti-cally naïve. Indeed, quite the opposite: taken in isolation they all had distinct merits and would have been considered attractive propositions even for the experienced, professional, uncovered writer.

Example 1: Land Securities

Date	Stock	Stock price (p)	Option series	Option bid price (p)	January option expiry
7.1.80	LSI	248	Jan. 260	3	23.1.80

With only twelve business days outstanding to expiry of the option, a naked writer might have been attracted by the relevant figures for this out-of-the-money option and written the Jan. 260 at a premium of three points per contract. (See Table 6.7.)

Table 6.7

Cash collateral requirements	Gross figures
25% of the stock closing price (248)	62
Less Difference between closing price and the exercise price (260 − 248)	12
	50
Less Premium taken	3
	47p per contract

This represents, at best, a gross return on cash invested of 6.4% over 2.5 weeks. The only problem was that, by the week beginning 21 January, the situation had been transformed as LSI shares shot up in an equity market that suddenly took off (FTI rose 50 points in two weeks). With only two days left to expiry of the option, the situation had changed dramatically!

Date	Stock	Stock price (p)	Option series	Option offer price (p)
21.1.80	LSI	286	Jan. 260	27

The option had risen ninefold against the uncovered writer, who would have been faced with the unpalatable prospect of buying back his written option at 27 or waiting to be exercised before buying the shares to meet his contractual obligation.

Example 2: General Electric Company

Date	Stock	Stock price (p)	Option series	Option bid price (p)	Expiry date
2.6.80	GEC	346	July 390	4	23.7.80

The not too aggressive uncovered writer may well have found the above situation an attractive risk. GEC's share price had been somewhat laggard, and a rise from 346 to 390 within three weeks did not seem all that likely, despite the fact that the company would announce its trading results before

106

expiry of the option. If the option expired worthless within three weeks (as seemed likely) the four points of premium received (gross) would have been equivalent to one half of the *annual* net dividend paid on the underlying shares. (See Table 6.8.)

Table 6.8

Cash collateral requirements	Gross figures
25% of the stock closing price (346)	86
Less Difference between the closing price (346) and the exercise price (390)	44
	42
Less Premium taken	4
	38p per contract

Accordingly, the maximum (gross) profit would have been 10.5% (4 on 38) over a time scale of 7.5 weeks. What a magnificent prospect! How unattractive it rendered the cash sitting on deposit with the clearing bank earning a mere 15% per annum (and taxed as unearned income)! The case was compelling, and the July 390 option was written at a premium of four, uncovered. The statistical progression in Table 6.9 unravels the horrifying saga of the savagery of the stock and option price movements which, technically, could lead the uncovered writer into the Bankruptcy Court.

Table 6.9

Date	Stock price (p)	July 390 offer price (p)
2.6.80	346	5
9.6.80	356	5
16.6.80	369	5
23.6.80	395	16½
30.6.80	402	25
7.7.80	432*	44
14.7.80	443	60
21.7.80	490	100

*Results announced 3.7.80.

By 21 July (just two days prior to expiry), the poor, uncovered writer was confronted with two daunting prospects: having to repurchase his written option at 100 (for a loss of 96 points per contract), and having to increase his cash collateral for the privilege of supporting his mounting losses. (See Table 6.10.)

Table 6.10

Cash collateral requirements	Gross figures
25% of the stock closing price (490)	122
Plus Difference between market price	
(490) and the exercise price (390)	100
	222p per contract

Example 3 or How to get five out of six right, and still lose money
Early in October 1979 an uncovered writer took the view that the market might break downwards from the FT Index 450–480 trading range in which it had gyrated all summer; but he was not 100 per cent sure! As a result, he was drawn to the heavy out-of-the-money option series on five stocks to implement his uncovered writing strategy, in the expectation that they would expire worthless in due course and render a most acceptable return on the capital employed (i.e. the cash collateral required). This view was re-inforced when he compared the level of the premiums offered (over a four-month time scale to expiry) with the annual dividend pay-out on the underlying shares (see Table 6.11). He wrote one contract on each series.

Table 6.11

Stock	Stock offer price (p)	Option series	Option bid price (p)	Dividend Gross	Net	Effective sale price (p)	% rise in shares required for the stock to be called
GEC	383	Jan. 420	17	11.5	8.0	437	9.7
GEC	383	Jan. 460	6	11.5	8.0	466	20.0
LSI	303	Jan. 330	10	11.0	7.7	340	8.9
CGF	264	Jan. 280	13	15.7	11.0	293	6.1
M & S	104	Jan. 110	6	4.5	3.2	116	5.7
RTZ	318	Nov. 360	7	20.0	14.0	367	13.2

We can trace the progress of the stocks/options over the weeks that followed.

Week beginning 22.10.79. Progressing well. Four out of the five stocks/ options had dropped sharply, but CGF had risen from 264 to 281 and the Jan. 280 series had risen from 13 to 18.

Week beginning 23.11.79. Market still falling. All option series were standing at purely nominal levels, with the exception of CGF which had jumped to 339 and the Jan. 280 which had almost quadrupled to 70.

Week beginning 17.12.79. Overall situation the same, but CGF now 377 and the Jan. 280 series 100.

Week beginning 21.1.80. Overall situation the same, but CGF now 480 and the Jan. 280 series had doubled to 200.

By the expiry date of the options, five out of the six series had wasted to zero (thus achieving maximum profitability) but CGF had risen from 264 to 480, and the Jan. 280 series had appreciated from 13 to 200, necessitating a closing purchase and a book loss of 187. The five successful options totalled 46 points, the unsuccessful CGF Jan. 280 series lost 187. The cash collateral required to cover the runaway CGF Jan. 280 would also have risen to horrifying levels as daily calls were being made. All in all, a total disaster, having read the market correctly and picked five out of six totally successful written options. Desperately unfair maybe, but that is what happened. It is consoling to realise that it is extremely unlikely (I sincerely hope) that any writer would have sat, almost mummified, while the disaster was unravelling, without taking remedial action a good deal earlier. Nevertheless, these examples illustrate (with frightening clarity) how financially devastating uncovered writing can be when the situation starts to go wrong.

Rules/mandatory survival kit for aspiring uncovered writers

(1) *Don't* write uncovered in-the-money options series, particularly in high volatility stocks, unless totally convinced that either the market as a whole (preferably) or an individual stock in question is due for a significant percentage fall.

(2) *Don't* write heavy out-of-the-money option series in high beta stocks unless the market looks very over-bought, irrespective of how statistically attractive (i.e. expensive) the option would appear to be.

(3) If an uncovered written option appears to be going wrong or is giving concern, close it immediately (by repurchasing it) and stomach any loss with good grace; there will be many more opportunities in the future. Being clinical and unemotional about cutting losses is easy to preach but difficult to effect. Human nature being what it is, the natural inclination for most investors is to be bullish (i.e. optimistic) in outlook. Writing 'naked' options which gives expression to a fairly aggressive bearish stance is often psychologically disturbing and can have one particularly dangerous side effect. Once the decision has been taken and the bear position effected, the problem appears to have been solved; the decision

must be correct, and it is simply a matter of time before potentiality converts to actuality. If the stock begins to defy gravity and perform contrary to expectations, there is a real danger that the writer, in almost total disbelief, becomes even more convinced that he is right and more entrenched in his view. This can have disastrous financial ramifications in option trading and *must* be corrected. To aid this task, I consider that the use of a system of price limits is fundamentally important as a tool designed to reduce the risks of substantial financial loss from this sphere of operation. The techniques of buy stop/stop loss orders are an integral part of the American investment scene but used relatively little in this country: hence, there has been little written discussion of their relevance and application.

Public limit orders

The London market operates a system of public limit orders. Any member of the public may, through a broker, enter a public limit order in a traded option series. Such orders must be specified as 'good until cancelled' (GTC) or 'good for the day only' (GD). GTC orders remain valid until withdrawn from the market. GD orders are valid only for the dealing day on which they are entered and are automatically cancelled at the close of business on that day. Limit orders constitute firm dealing instructions. They are entered on special forms and handed to a board dealer who is obligated to execute them immediately they become practicable.

A public limit order at a stipulated price is given priority over any other deal in the relevant option series, except in circumstances where this priority would prevent the execution of a 'spread order' without enabling the public limit order to be executed. Public limit orders are cancelled only when the broker who placed the limit form with the board dealer has asked the board dealer to return the form to him. Unless the limit form has been withdrawn from the board dealer, the order may be executed at any time. It is essential that members of the public are fully cognisant of this procedure, since there must inevitably be an interval of time, however brief, between the receipt of a client's instructions to withdraw a limit from the market, and the actual physical withdrawal of the limit form from the board dealer. If, during this interval, the limit has been executed, the resulting bargain will stand and will be reversed only by a further transaction in the market.

In my opinion, the aspiring writer of uncovered options should familiarise himself thoroughly with the concept of price limits: indeed, they should become a cornerstone of his strategy. The object of the exercise is to limit any potential loss by being 'short' to a figure less than the amount of the required margin investment. This system enables the writer, in normal market conditions, to cancel a short position by buying back the option at a predetermined price if the shares start rising. In these circumstances, the uncovered writer would instruct his broker to place price limits GTC or GD with the board dealer in the relevant security when the premium of a particular series reached a predetermined level. However, it should be reiterated that such price limits cannot be effective in conditions where a price movement is sudden and substantial, reflecting, for example, a take-over bid or unexpected company news.

Another method used to limit the magnitude of potential loss is to close out the short position when the underlying shares reach a predetermined level. American experience of option trading reveals that the use of premium limits is by far the more common of the two, although the latter has decided uses, particularly when writing heavy out-of-the-money calls. However, in the London Option Market there is the restriction that limit orders cannot be made conditional upon the price of the underlying security or on any other contingent circumstance. Contingency orders may not be entered as public limit orders.

As I have already indicated, the importance of the use of price limits by the uncovered writer cannot be over-stressed. A good broker should offer to execute GTC limit orders based on the price of the underlying share price reaching a predetermined level upon receipt of written instructions so to do.

Premium price limits
This is much the more precise strategy for accurately limiting predetermined losses. A writer sells an IMP Aug. 80 call when the shares are 85, receiving a premium of six points. If he decides to restrict his re-purchase price to a level roughly equating to the premiums received, he would place a price limit of around 12 on the prospective premium level. If he simply limits the price rise of the underlying shares to around 91, there is no guarantee that the premium will not be more than the anticipated 12 points. Indeed, there is every likelihood that the premium will have increased by

an additional amount as investors, having witnessed a sharp upward movement to date, begin to anticipate a further extension of the rise. As a general rule, therefore, the investor writing at-the-money and in-the-money calls should employ premium limits to protect his upside loss exposure.

Underlying share price limits

The main difficulty in utilising this method lies in adjudicating at which level to place the price limit. A very low 'safety first' figure will certainly guarantee a small resultant loss on repurchase, but will often close out a call that subsequently expires worthless. On the other hand, a high price limit placed on a heavy out-of-the-money call may turn out very costly if the share price starts moving up and suddenly begins to approach the exercise price. As I stressed earlier, the most important factor in writing uncovered calls is to protect against a runaway short position. Hence, the cautious employment of low price limits will be favoured by those wishing to guarantee small losses on written calls that begin to look wrong. This policy *must* be adopted by investors writing low-premium out-of-the-money calls on volatile shares. Assume that IMP shares stand at 68 with six weeks remaining of an 80 strike price call. A rise in the price of the shares to 71 will probably have little upward impact on the premium itself. However, if the price rises toward the exercise price, the call will move up noticeably quicker for every point increase in the shares. If the shares reach the exercise price and continue rising, then the option premium will rise almost point-for-point in unison. The trader prepared to assume higher risks and ride out what he believes is simply an upward correction in a downphase will place a limit at one or two points beneath the exercise pice.

(4) Spread the risk by diversifying the portfolio of calls written, no matter how attractive the return offered on any one particular option.
(5) Analyse the underlying security in detail before writing calls on it. Review the historical financial record and assess current and future prospects in an attempt to measure intrinsic value. Monitor how the share price has reacted to major market movements in the past to ascertain relative volatility. Do not labour under the misapprehension that the option market offers a substitute for conventional analysis and financial projection. The two are complementary and not competitive.

(6) No adjustment is made to the exercise price of the option when the underlying shares are marked 'ex dividend'. From the writer's standpoint, this can result in a valuable reduction in the price of the shares. Dividend declaration dates and 'ex dividend' dates are thus important considerations in the timing of writing calls.

(7) Trading options is time consuming. The immense volatility of market price movements over the past few years is, in my view, likely to continue. Within this framework, a limited life option can gyrate rapidly over a relatively short period of time, and thus requires a flexible trading mentality rather than a long-term investment attitude in its implementation.

(8) Don't be greedy. Aim to make a specific return on capital employed and, if the target is attained, particularly if achieved ahead of schedule, take it with gratitude.

(9) Don't job backwards in option trading, particularly to bemoan missed opportunities: if you do, you will end up dispirited and disillusioned.

7

Spreads and hedges, part II

BEAR SPREADS

The last part of Chapter 6 was devoted to the risks and rewards of writing uncovered call options and, as such, highlighted the dual problems of potential unlimited loss on the upside and rocketing collateral demands when the position begins to go wrong. A *bear spread* offers a partial solution to both of these problems but, in so doing, reduces proportionately the maximum profitability derived from a successful uncovered write. Quite naturally, one cannot seek a measure of protection without forgoing some of the alternative gain.

At its most simple the bear spread technique involves the sale of a heavy-premium in-the-money option (to accommodate the bearish case) and the simultaneous purchase of either a marginally in-the-money series or, preferably, a low-premium, marginally out-of-the-money series (the 'insurance policy' in case the underlying share rises rather than falls as planned). If the underlying share subsequently falls to or below the exercise price of the written option either before or at expiry, both options will waste to zero, but the 'profit' on the written 'bear' will more than accommodate the smaller loss from the purchased option position. If the share price rises rather than falls, the marginally out-of-the-money bull position should largely keep pace with the losses on the written in-the-money option: in all probability, a small loss will result from this transaction once allowance has been made for all the expenses, which is neither too surprising nor too penal for having read the movement of the stock price totally wrongly. Compare the horrendous position that the uncovered writer faces for committing such a cardinal sin!

The bear spread is also kinder in the demands it makes on cash margining. This works out according to the following formula: the difference between the two strike prices of the option series used to effect the spread *less* the credit from the spread itself. Two examples are appropriate at this juncture.

Example 1: ICI

Date	Stock	Stock price (p)	July 390 bid price (p)	July 420 offer price (p)
7.7.80	ICI	391	8	1½

ICI's share price performance, relative to a strong equity market, had been poor. An investor, reading the market over-bought and on the look-out for bear spreads, alighted on the ICI July 390/420 situation with just two weeks remaining to expiry. It looked attractive.

Maximum liability on the spread (420 − 390)	30
Sold the spread for (8 − 1½)	6½
Spread margin requirement (30 − 6½)	23½

The arithmetic of the spread (ten contracts), after full expenses, is given in Table 7.1. By the July expiry date, ICI shares had dropped to 374 and both options wasted to zero. The following day the investor received a cheque for £3,000 (£591.90 for the spread premium plus £2,408.10 for the cash margin cover).

His profit was thus £591.90 on a capital outlay of £2,408.10, i.e. 24.6%, over two weeks.

Table 7.1

7/7 − 10 ICI July 330 at 8	£800		7/7 + 10 ICI July 420 at 1½	£150	
10 × £1.50	£15.00		10 × £1.50	£15.00	
2.5% commission	£20.00		S/C	—	
VAT	£ 5.25		VAT	£ 2.25	
C/S	£ 0.30		C/S	£ 0.30	
	£40.55	£759.45		£17.55	£167.55

Net credit from spread £759.45 − £167.55 = £591.90.
Cash margin required £3,000 − £591.90 = £2,408.10.

Example 2: Courtaulds

Date	Stock	Stock price (p)	July 70 bid price (p)	July 80 offer price (p)	July 90 offer price (p)
7.7.80	CTD	87	16	8½	1½

Another investor, also reading the general market heavily over-bought at this time and mistrusting the uncharacteristic sharp rise in the CTD share price, felt sufficiently bearish to write the July 70/80 bear spread for 7.5 points.

Maximum liability on the spread (80 – 70)	10
Sold spread for (16 – 8½)	7½
Spread margin requirement	2½

By the July expiry date (23/7), the CTD share price had collapsed to 68; the July 70s, 80s and 90s all expired worthless. The arithmetic of the spread (again using ten contracts), after full expenses is shown in Table 7.2.

Table 7.2

7/7 – 10 CTD July 70 at 16	£1,600		7/7 + 10 CTD July 80 at 8½	£850
10 × £1.50	£15.00		10 × £1.50	£15.00
2.5% commission	£40.00		S/C	—
VAT	£ 8.25		VAT	£ 2.25
C/S	£ 0.30		C/S	£ 0.30
	£63.55 £1,536.45			£17.55 £867.55

Net credit from spread £1,536.45 – £867.55 = £668.90.
Cash margin requirement £1,000 – £668.90 = £331.10.
   Thus, return on capital employed was 102% over two weeks.

I suggested earlier that a bear spread, executed (on the purchase side) by courtesy of a marginally out-of-the-money option series, would probably result in a small loss (after all expenses) if the underlying security rose rather than fell. The reason for this is, quite simply, that the deep in-the-money bear position will rise faster than the out-of-the-money bull position. Either one of two steps can be taken to reduce the extent of this potential loss:

(1) purchase a marginally in-the-money call option rather than an out-of-the-money call (see the Courtaulds example above); or
(2) effect a variable-ratio bear spread by purchasing two out-of-the-money calls.

VARIABLE-RATIO BEAR SPREADS

The example of Courtaulds used earlier will suffice again to illustrate the principle of a variable-ratio bear spread.

Date	Stock	Stock price (p)	July 80 bid price (p)	July 90 offer price (p)
7.7.80	CTD	87	8½	1½

The same investor, bearish of the general level of the market but wishing to avoid the risks of a further sharp upward movement in the CTD share price, might have effected a variable-ratio bear spread by selling ten contracts of the

July 80s at 8½ and purchasing twice the number (i.e. 20 contracts) of the July 90 series. The arithmetic of the transaction, after all expenses, is shown in Table 7.3.

Table 7.3

− 10 CTD July 80 at 8½		£850	+ 20 CTD July 90 at 1½		£300
10 × £1.50	£15.00		20 × £1.50	£30.00	
2.5% commission	£21.25		*Min. commission	£ 5.00	
VAT	£ 5.44		VAT	£ 5.25	
C/S	£ 0.30		C/S	£ 0.30	
	£41.99	£808.01		£40.55	£340.55

Net credit from spread £808.01 − £340.55 = £467.46.
Maximum cash liability on spread (90 − 80) = £1,000.00 (10 contracts).
Sold spread for (8½ − 3) £467.46.
Spread margin requirement (10 − 5½) = £532.54.
*S/C applicable to 10 contracts.

Let's take the hypothetical case that, instead of collapsing to 68 as, indeed, the CTD shares did at expiry of the July option (23/7), they had actually risen to, say, 97. The investor would thus close his bear position (July 80s) by re-purchasing the option at its intrinsic value of 17 (80 + 17) and selling his July 90 options at their intrinsic value of 7 (90 + 7). The net arithmetic of the exercise is given in Table 7.4.

Table 7.4

+ 10 CTD July 80 at 17		£1,700	− 20 CTD July 90 at 7		£1,400
10 × £1.50	£15.00		20 × £1.50	£30.00	
2.5% commission	£42.50		2.5% commission		
			on £700	£17.50	
VAT	£ 8.63		VAT	£ 7.13	
C/S	£ 0.30		C/S	£ 0.30	
	£66.43	£1,766.43		£54.93	£1,345.07

Net debit from spread £1,766.43 − £1,345.07 = £421.36.
Hence, net profit on transaction £467.46 − £421.36 = £46.10

Readers in the process of turning up their noses at this relatively low profit should reflect that this was a result of reading the stock market movement in CTD underlying share price completely wrongly (remember that we are discussing a hypothetical example). If the share price had risen beyond 97 by expiry, the profit on the transaction would have been proportionately greater – the bull position would have been rising twice as fast as the bear. The Traded Options Market thus enables the investor to be 100 per cent wrong about the share price and still end up making a profit!

8

The dealing system

INTRODUCTION

It will by now be evident that the concept of a traded option is totally different from that of the underlying security and, for this reason, a special dealing system is required to meet the needs of the market.

In every class of option there will normally be at least six series, sometimes twelve or more, according to the movement of the price of the underlying security, and consequently a great deal of information must be immediately available in order that trading decisions may be taken. Moreover, because traded options are an instrument for the modification of portfolio risk, and thus demand a small capital outlay in relation to the risks assumed, it is important that participation in the market should be as widespread as possible in order that every shade of view about the underlying security may be reflected. These requirements dictate that the market should be based on an auction system of bids and offers made in open competition, and that there should be a facility whereby members of the public can enter firm limits, either as buyers or sellers, in the certain knowledge that these orders will have priority over all other business at their stipulated price.

STRUCTURE OF THE MARKET

(1) The traded options market is situated on the floor of the London Stock Exchange.

(2) *Trading hours*
Trading will take place only on designated pitches on the floor of the Stock Exchange between 9.35 a.m. and 3.30 p.m. No after-hours dealing is permitted, and telephone transactions are strictly prohibited.

(3) *Open outcry market*

Dealing in traded options is by 'open outcry'. The market in each class of options is made by a 'crowd', consisting of a board dealer, market makers and brokers, trading openly with each other. Each 'crowd' is controlled by the board dealer who acts as referee.

(4) *Participants*

All member firms of the Stock Exchange may deal in traded options. Firms who are not clearing members must settle business in traded options through a clearing agent. Each non-clearing member must register the name of his clearing agent with the London Option Clearing House (LOCH) before trading. In addition to acting as agents, brokers may deal as principals for their own account. They may also act as market makers under Rule 94.

Jobbers may act as board dealers and/or market makers, subject to registration by the Council.

Jobbers who are not registered board dealers or market makers may only deal in traded options on those underlying securities for which they are registered under Rule 91, and may not quote a two-way price; firms of jobbers who wish to deal in traded options in classes in which they are not registered under Rule 91 as dealers in the underlying security must deal through a broker.

(5) *Role of the board dealer*

The function of the board dealer is to:
- (i) ensure that an orderly market is conducted in the 'crowd' for which he is responsible;
- (ii) accept public limit orders and ensure that the execution of public limits in his care takes precedence over all other business at the price;
- (iii) establish opening and closing prices;
- (iv) display information relevant to the series in his charge;
- (v) be prepared to quote a price at all times in at least one contract of each option series in his charge. This price should not normally be wider than that prevailing in the underlying security;
- (vi) intervene as principal when a broker or brokers wish to match orders;
- (vii) ensure that he or an approved deputy is present at all times during trading hours.

Board dealers are appointed annually by the Council of the Stock

Exchange, who may at their absolute discretion remove a board dealer at any time if he fails to discharge his duties in a satisfactory manner.

(6) *Role of the market maker*

Market makers are required by the Council to make a market in at least two option classes, and must make prices in at least one contract of each series in those classes on the same terms as the board dealer. Market makers may, without such obligation, also trade in other classes.

Market makers must be available in the market during trading hours.

Market makers may deal only as principals, and may not conduct agency business.

Those brokers who also act as market makers under Rule 94 will be required to keep separate their market making and agency business, and employ separate personnel to perform these functions.

Such brokers may only execute their client's business with their own market maker if the board dealer decides that there is no other way in which the business can be transacted.

(7) *'Public' orders*

An order received by a broker on behalf of a client is known as a 'public' order (as opposed to an 'in-house' order). 'Public' orders take priority over 'in-house' orders and the business of board dealers and market makers.

(8) *'In-house' orders*

Brokers dealing on behalf of their own or another member firm acting as principal; or for partners, members or employees of their own or another member firm; or for any dealing companies controlled by such persons, must declare the business as 'in-house' to the board dealer before dealing. 'In-house' orders are not entitled to priority of execution over other business in the 'crowd'.

An 'in-house' order which cannot be executed immediately may, by private arrangement, be left in the custody of a market maker, who will declare it to the crowd and endeavour to execute it as soon as it becomes practicable.

(9) *The dealing procedure*

At the commencement of the day's trading, the board dealer must call over in rotation the prices of the series in each class in his charge, until all possible public limit orders have been executed and a trading level is established.

During the call-over no dealings are permitted in any series other than that being called over at that time.

The board dealer will not accept public limit orders to participate in the call-over any later than 9.35 a.m. Public limits may be withdrawn at any time except during the call-over. After the call-over in all series is completed, the board dealer may accept public limit orders at any time prior to the closing call-over.

A broker, having received a client's order, must approach the board dealer and ask the price in a voice loud enough to be heard by all present in the 'crowd'. The board dealer and market makers must then call out their prices in voices loud enough to be heard by all in the 'crowd'.

Prices quoted by the board dealers and market makers shall be good for any other member of the 'crowd' if the broker requesting the price does not deal. A broker who has asked a price from the 'crowd' has the right to deal with each and every member of the 'crowd' at the price which that member has made to him in response to his request. If, however, a broker, having heard the prices which the members of the 'crowd' have made to him, elects to challenge the 'crowd' at a different price, then the members of the 'crowd' are immediately released from their obligation to deal and may alter their quotation.

Once a bargain has been agreed, the broker to it must complete the official dealing slip, ensuring that all copies are validated by the appropriate time stamp.

The board dealer must close the market each day by calling over in rotation the prices of the series in each class in his charge. The closing call-over establishes the prices on which LOCH calculates margin requirements.

(10) *Dealing prices*
The smallest permitted price fraction in traded option bargains is ¼p.

(11) *Execution of an order in the market*
Example: A client has submitted an order to a broker to buy six XYZ July 420s at best.

The broker's dealer will go to the XYZ pitch, where he will see the price of the underlying security, the latest quotation of all the option series currently listed, and, for each series, the prices and sizes of the public limit orders which are closest to the market quotation.

The situation in XYZ July 420s might be as follows:

Last market quotation	16–18
Last trade executed at	17

Public limit orders showing
a buyer of 15 contracts at   15½
and a seller of 10 contracts at 18

The broker will realise at once that he can execute his order by buying six of the ten contracts offered on the public limit order by the board dealer at 18p, but he will try to improve on this price.

Broker: 'What are July 420s?'
Board dealer: '16½–18.'
1st market maker: '16½–17½.'
2nd market maker: '16½–17½.'
Broker: 'I'll give you 17 for six contracts.'
1st market maker: 'Offer you six at 17½.'
2nd market maker: 'Offer you three at 17¼.'
Broker: 'I'll buy your three at 17¼ and give the same price for another three.'
No further reaction from the 'crowd'.
Broker to 'crowd': 'I'll bid 17½ for the other three.'
2nd market maker: 'Sell you the other three at 17½.'

The broker has now completed his order, having bought three contracts at 17¼p and three at 17½p. The whole conversation between the participants was conducted in tones loud enough to be heard by the whole 'crowd' on the pitch, so that everyone had an opportunity to compete for the broker's business. The board dealer was obviously not anxious to sell any options himself because, although the best public limit buying order was only at 15½p, he was willing to bid 16½p for his own book, but he declined to offer options at a price cheaper than the public limit selling order which he was holding at 18p. The price display will now be altered to reflect the latest business.

(12) *Dealing priority*
If more than one member of the 'crowd' is bidding or offering at the same price in response to a request by a broker, priority is given to any other broker with a public order. If no broker wishes to execute the public order at the price, then that member of the 'crowd' who last traded at that price or worse takes priority. When no member of the 'crowd' wishes to claim priority, then the board dealer will split the transaction between those members of the 'crowd' who wish to trade at the price.

(13) *Public limit orders*
Any non-contingent public order which cannot be executed immediately may be passed to the board dealer and entered as a public limit

order. Such orders must be specified as 'good until cancelled' (GTC) or 'good for the day only' (GD). GTC orders remain valid until physically withdrawn from the market. GD orders are valid only for the dealing day on which they are entered, and are automatically cancelled at the close of business on that day.

The board dealer or any member of the 'crowd' may execute a public limit order by undertaking a transaction with the board dealer at the stipulated price of the limit order. The board dealer must then execute another transaction at that price with the broker who placed the public limit order. The open outcry principle must be observed in all dealings.

Public limit orders at the same price will be executed in order of receipt by the board dealer as indicated by the time stamp.

A board dealer or market maker who has executed a public limit order shall have priority in executing the next public limit order in the same series. Public limit orders take priority over all other business in the market at their stipulated prices.

A public limit order cannot be made conditional upon the price of the underlying security or on any other contingent circumstance. A public limit order constitutes a firm dealing instruction. It must be entered on a dealing slip, time-stamped and handed to the board dealer, who is obligated to execute it immediately it becomes practicable.

A public limit order is only cancelled when the broker who placed the limit slip with the board dealer has asked the board dealer to return the slip to him. Unless the limit slip has been physically withdrawn from the board dealer, the order may be executed at any time.

The following conditions govern the entry of public limit orders.

(i) They must be entered on the dealing slips.
(ii) They must be firm and marked GD or GTC.
(iii) They must be time-stamped when lodged with the board dealer.
(iv) They can be cancelled only by being physically withdrawn.
(v) Contingent orders may not be entered as public limit orders.

Where any event occurs which involves amendment to the terms of contracts in a class, all outstanding GTC limits are deemed to lapse on the morning the stock is quoted 'ex' and must be re-submitted by the broker responsible.

(14) *Trading halts*

A board dealer must call a temporary halt to trading in a particular class of options when:

(i) in his opinion, prices of the series in that class are moving too fast for public limit orders to be executed in an orderly manner;

(ii) trading in the underlying security has been halted or suspended.

A board dealer may also call a temporary halt to trading in a particular class of options when unusual conditions or circumstances obtain.

The board dealer or an approved deputy must remain on the pitch during the period of the halt.

A trading halt is indicated by the board dealer sounding a buzzer and illuminating a light above the pitch.

The board dealer may be called upon to justify his action to the Council of the Stock Exchange.

(15) *Trading information*

LOCH publishes on every business day the number of contracts traded on the previous day in each series of traded options, together with the total number of contracts open in each class (i.e. 'the open interest'). This information, together with the closing price of each option series, is available to all participants.

9

Taxation treatment of traded options

HISTORY AND FISCAL BACKGROUND

Both before the Traded Options Market commenced operations and for much of its early life, the medium was plagued and unnecessarily hindered by discussion and commentary, much of which was speculative and ill-informed. That is not to say that there were not considerable fiscal obstacles to surmount. The history of the Inland Revenue's distrust of all options dates from the early 1960s, when a number of ingenious tax-avoidance schemes were set up involving the creation of purely fictitious options. Although these had nothing to do with the securities industry, they were unfortunately next in line for new legislation when the Capital Gains Tax (CGT) was introduced in 1965: the Revenue thus took the opportunity to tag the 'wasting assets' provisions on to the Finance Act, and in so doing penalised all option transactions. By 1970 they had been persuaded that such draconian measures were not necessary in the case of listed warrants, and the legislation was amended accordingly. Unfortunately, insufficient pressure was put on them at the same time by the option lobby to seek similar relaxation to Stock Exchange options.

It is worth bearing in mind that the Inland Revenue were influenced in their deliberations by two arguments. Firstly, the tax calculations in the case of a warrant which was traded actively (i.e. National Westminster) were extremely complicated; and secondly, and more important, the fact that the existence of an active market clearly made the contention that an option transaction might be purely fictitious a ludicrous proposition.

The problems were indeed considerable, but much of the early com-

126

ment, suggesting that the London Traded Options Market had no chance of survival without a change in the prevailing legislation, was too simplistic, negative and misleading. For example, it failed to reflect a realistic analysis of the comparative costs involved. To take an example, suppose that ICI stands in the market at 390 with the equivalent six-month at-the-money option quoted at 20p. A buyer of the option who sold again after three months would have 'wasted' 10p gross, which would cost him, one way or another, 3p net. On the other hand, the buyer of the shares for a similar time scale would actually have paid 7.8p in transfer stamp, and the capital gains tax offset would reduce this to a net 5.5p. Thus, although the wasting asset treatment was most certainly unfair, unreasonable and unviable, it was less so than the stamp duty, so far as the short- to medium-term trader was concerned.

Nevertheless, the prevailing gains tax provisions created problems, at the heart of which was the Inland Revenue ruling that options have no underlying value (including in-the-money series) and, as a result, cannot be regarded as 'securities' for tax purposes: hence, they were treated as wasting assets. Representations were thus made to the Board of the Inland Revenue in an attempt to effect consistent, logical and, above all, equitable changes to the legislation. The fiscal objectives of such representations were to establish that taxable profits should be equal to the actual gain derived from transactions, with full relief for those transactions which yielded a loss. While the historical legislation is open to differing interpretation, it can be summarised as follows.

(1) Purchasing call options

(a) If a call option was not exercised, the option was abandoned and the ensuing loss was not allowable as a capital gains tax loss: it was not considered as a disposal, but rather that its CGT cost had 'wasted' to nil.

(b) If the call option was exercised, the cost of the option was added to the cost of the shares acquired, so that CGT relief was obtained when the shares were subsequently sold.

(c) If the call option was sold (i.e. closing sale transaction) before the due expiry date, then the wasting asset provisions would apply to the cost of acquisition, so that the taxable gains exceed the actual gains.

Admittedly, as 1 (b) reveals, it was possible within the framework of the existing rules to obtain full relief for the cost of the call option by exercising the option, taking up the shares and subsequently re-selling them. However, this was clearly contrary to the main *raison d'être* behind the establishing of a secondary market, which by its very structure is designed to avoid this somewhat laborious and costly process.

Clearly, the former rules were, in part, both illogical and inequitable, and needed amending in the context of a market in traded options. Option transactions conducted through an option exchange had to be accorded comparable treatment to that applied to share warrants under Section 58 Finance Act 1971. In particular (i) the abandonment or lapse of an option should constitute a disposal thereof, and (ii) the wasting asset provisions should not be applied.

(2) Writing call options

(a) If the option was exercised and the shares were delivered to the purchaser, the option money received was added to the sale proceeds for CGT purposes.

(b) If the option was not exercised, the proceeds were treated as a capital gain and were taxed as such.

(c) If the option was closed by the purchase of another option with the same maturity date and strike price (in the secondary market), the payment so made was not an allowable cost against the premium proceeds received. In other words, CGT was chargeable on the premium proceeds, while the consideration for the purchase was considered to be a separate deal to which rule 1 (a) above would apply.

Clearly, rule 2 (c) needed amending. A re-acquisition in such instances (i.e. closing purchase transaction) should be identified with the original disposal for tax purposes, so that only the net gain or loss came within the scope of capital gains tax.

After much exhortation and pleading (particularly on the part of the members of the Options Committee of the London Stock Exchange) the first fiscal breakthrough was made:

A traded option is currently treated as a wasting asset (Section 138 (2) of the Capital Gains Tax Act) with the result that its cost of acquisition is written down progressively throughout the period it is held: only the balance remaining at the time of its disposal can be set against the sale proceeds in computing any capital gain or loss which may have accrued. *It is proposed to* bring the treatment of traded options into line with that of share warrants. Where, therefore, a traded option is disposed of after 5

April 1980, the wasting asset treatment will not be applied and so the full cost of acquisition will be taken into account in the capital gains tax computation. Furthermore, the abandonment of a traded option will be treated as a disposal (at present Section 137 (4) of the Capital Gains Tax Act prevents this).

(Inland Revenue Press Release, 26 March 1980)

Success, at long last, as traded options were given fiscal parity with warrants and, most important, the open announcement of these structural changes by the Chancellor of the Exchequer in his Budget speech gave the traded options market official Government blessing and hence increased credibility.

Regrettably (mainly due to a technical misunderstanding of the subject matter), the amendments announced at this time did not clarify the position of the covered (or uncovered) writer repurchasing his option (to close). At the end of March 1980 I wrote:

Following consultation with the IR I am by no means satisfied that their interpretation of the fiscal treatment of a written option which is subsequently repurchased at a loss shows the qualities of consistency, logic and equity which have been applied to a straightforward purchase and sale. My contention all along has been that the simplest way of solving this problem is to identify the closing purchase transaction with the original disposal for tax purposes so that only the net gain or loss comes within the scope of the capital gains tax.

It took a further six months of verbal 'battle' before this point was conceded; but conceded it was, finally.

Thus, while the present taxation treatment of traded options (these rules do not necessarily apply to traditional options) should be clear from the above paragraphs, I will set out below the position for each transaction so that there can be no possible confusion.

PRESENT TAX POSITION

(A) Private individuals

Overall, the CGT position of traded option transactions (for private individuals) is identical to that of any other 'security' or 'investment'. The broad principles are as follows:

(1) Options are specifically declared to be assets for the purpose of CGT.
(2) Current London traded options are excluded from the wasting asset rules which existed prior to 6 April 1980.

(3) Traded option contracts of the same series are fungible assets and as such are subject to the pooling rules which apply to ordinary shares.

(4) When shares are acquired by exercising a call option, the cost of the option is treated as part of the cost of buying the shares. For example:

> Purchase one ICI July 360 call at 23
> Exercise into the stock at 360
> Book cost of purchase 360 + 23 = 383

Likewise when shares are disposed of by exercising a put option the cost of the option is deductible from the sale proceeds.

(5) When shares are disposed of in satisfaction of a writer's obligations under a call option, the option premium is treated as part of the proceeds of selling the shares. For example:

> Write one ICI July 360 at 20
> Option exercised against at 360
> Selling price of underlying share 360 + 20 = 380

Likewise when shares are acquired in satisfaction of a writer's obligations under a put option, the option premium is treated as reducing the price which he pays for the shares.

(6) In a letter to the Stock Exchange dated 20 January 1981, the Inland Revenue have agreed that the holder of a London traded option should be regarded as acquiring the shares called (or disposing of the shares put) on the business day following the day he exercises his options. As a result they will be identified with any similar shares sold (or bought) on that following day. Likewise the writer of a London traded option who receives an exercise notice should be regarded as disposing of the shares called or acquiring the shares put on the day on which the notice was assigned to him.

(7) The chargeable gain or allowable loss will simply be the difference between cost and proceeds. An allowable loss resulting from a lapsed purchase contract is deemed to accrue on the option expiry date.

(8) The writing of a traded option is treated as a disposal of an asset which cost nothing; this rule is displaced if the option is exercised.

(9) Where a written contract lapses at expiry, the whole of the proceeds are chargeable to CGT and the chargeable gain is

deemed to arise on the day on which the option is written. If an option is still current when the tax year ends, the writer must report in his tax return the chargeable gain which was deemed to arise when he wrote the contract. This rule is displaced if he subsequently receives notice of exercise.

If a writer closes his position by buying a call contract of the same series (or limits his position by buying a contract of a different series), then, if both contracts lapse, he will be chargeable on the proceeds of writing his contract and will get an allowable loss equal to the cost of the closing purchase. The chargeable gain will be deemed to have arisen on the day the contract was written, but the allowable loss will not be deemed to accrue until the expiry date for contract of that series. This may well fall into the next tax year.

(B) Investment trusts and authorised unit trusts

In his April 1980 Budget, the Chancellor of the Exchequer abolished all capital gains tax within investment trusts and unit trust portfolios and transferred the entire liability to the shareholders. So for the first time since the famous Budget of 1965, trusts are completely free of any taxes on capital profits. In a letter to the Stock Exchange dated 24 September 1981 the Inland Revenue have confirmed that option transactions would not be regarded as a trading activity, in normal circumstances.

Following hard upon the Budget amendments (but after two years of negotiation), the Department of Trade and the unit trust trustees allowed unit trusts to enter the traded options market. The main rules under which they can operate are as follows.

(1) Only new unit trusts can write or purchase call options without reference to unit holders. Existing unit trusts are obliged to call a unit holders' meeting to apply for consent.

(2) Unit trusts which write options will have to write only *covered* options, i.e. they have to be able to deliver the underlying security on which the options have been written.

(3) Existing unit trusts will not be able to write options beyond the limit of 50 per cent of the total market values of their portfolio. However, there is no such limit for new trusts.

(4) Where option purchases are concerned, not more than 25 per cent of an existing fund can be set aside for options, and the

131

managers will be obligated at all times to hold enough cash to be able to exercise their options fully.

(C) Charities

A gain arising to a charity is exempt from CGT if it is used for charitable purposes. Because a traded option was formerly classed as a wasting asset, it was possible for a chargeable gain to arise even where an actual loss was sustained on the disposal. The Inland Revenue have, however, confirmed that the chargeable gain will be regarded as exempt, provided that:

(1) an actual gain from the same transaction would have been applicable and applied for charitable purposes;
(2) all income and capital distributions have previously been wholly for accepted charitable purposes; and
(3) both the acquisition and disposal of the asset concerned can be demonstrated as not being other than actions which bona fide charity trustees would have taken.

(D) Pension funds

Only pension funds remain the 'problem child' up to the time of writing. Although an approved superannuation fund is not charged to tax in respect of capital gains arising from the disposal of investments held as part of the fund, an Inland Revenue ruling in 1979 via Spicer & Pegler declared that an option, whether traded or otherwise, is not an 'investment' for the purposes of Section 21 (7) of the 1970 Finance Act. Nevertheless (in a letter to the Stock Exchange dated 24 September 1981) they stated that they will not normally regard a transaction in options by pension fund trustees as an adventure in the nature of trade (and hence profits would be chargeable to income tax under Schedule D). Hence, the proceeds from writing a contract which remained unexercised would be liable to capital gains tax. Furthermore, where a written option is exercised, the purchase of the stock in the market to meet the contractual liability to deliver does not classify as a tax-exempt transaction. It is only when the pension fund has written a covered option, which is subsequently exercised against it and the underlying stock delivered, that the normal tax exemption rules apply: this transaction clearly meets the criteria of a 'disposal of investments' held as part of the fund.

At present, the tax position regarding options is likened to that of warrants and nil paid provisional letters of allotment purchased in the market. For their interpretation of what is or is not an 'investment', the Inland Revenue rely on the decisions of the House of Lords in *CIR* v. *Tootal Broadhurst Lee Company Limited* and *Electrical Musical Industries Limited* v. *CIR*.

Because of these fiscal interpretations, pension funds find themselves at a competitive disadvantage in the Traded Options Market against authorised unit trusts and investment trusts. At the time of writing, the majority appear to be extremely reticent about rectifying this state of affairs. It is fiscally illogical and inequitable that the conservative attempt at a genuine disposal of stock held at a predetermined price should be penalised if that goal is not achieved (because the stock price falls below the strike price of the option). Likewise, because of their sheer size, pension funds' investment policy is geared (in theory at least) to acquiring stock on falling prices. In an endeavour to effect this strategy, writing put options offers an intelligent, conservative and flexible alternative approach. Is it logical or equitable therefore to penalise such an attempt if it fails simply because the shares rise in price (and are therefore not put on the writer)? Again, what realistic distinction can be drawn between the acceptance of underwriting fees and a subsequent purchase of the shares at an agreed price to meet the contractual liability, and the receipt of an option premium from a written put and the subsequent acquisition of the shares at the strike price?

There is now no good reason why these 'historic' interpretations should not be re-examined and amended. Much of the spade work has already been done and much has been achieved. It is now up to the managers of pension funds through their associations to take up their case. It is my wish that this book will encourage them to do just that. They will not regret the effort!

10

Trading put options

The object of this section of the book is to discuss the basic principles involved in trading put options, in the capacity both of a buyer and of a seller. I consider it most important that readers are familiar with the concept and structure of puts and are able to appreciate some of the advantages of using them strategically. The London Traded Options Market had been in existence for more than three years before the first put options were listed. Puts on Racal, Lonrho and BP were introduced on 28 May 1981; Grand Metropolitan Hotels and ICI on 23 July 1981; Consolidated Goldfields and RTZ on 21 September 1981; Vaal Reef puts and calls on 2 October 1981; Imperial Tobacco on 29 October 1981; GEC on 23 November 1981 and Barclays Bank on 28 January 1982.

Put options on the remaining seven classes could be introduced as soon as possible. At the time of writing, the London Traded Options Market is sufficiently well established to render illogical the trading of call options on any class without the corresponding puts. The introduction of Vaal Reef witnessed the simultaneous listing of call and put options; this development has presumably (it is to be hoped) set a precedent for future action as new classes are gradually added.

BUYING PUT OPTIONS

The buyer of a put option will require the right to sell 1,000 shares of a particular company at a specific price (exercise price) at any time up to and including the expiry date of the option. In essence, of course, the concept, mechanism, structure and strategies involved in buying a traded put option will vary little from those involved in purchasing a listed call option. The choice of put option will still vary between the

134

at-, in- and out-of-the-money categories, while differing premium values will again reflect the varying time scale involved and the volatility of the underlying security.

The fundamental difference, of course, between puts and calls is the direction over which the underlying share price is projected over the time scale of the option (i.e. *down* rather than *up*). The premiums on put options will also be somewhat lower than their call option counterparts, reflecting their comparative lack of popularity and the fact that their downside potential is more limited (i.e. the underlying stock can only fall from x to zero), whereas the potential gain from a traded call option is theoretically unlimited.

What then are the attractions and advantages of traded put options for both the investor holding the underlying security and the investor who does not? It is probably easier to deal with the second category first.

As I have already shown, the investor wishing to accommodate a downward projection in an underlying share price, without holding the underlying security, is limited to writing call options uncovered. This strategy has certain advantages but it requires (often considerable) cash collateral, provides limited maximum gain (the size of the option premium) and can be excessively costly if it goes wrong. Put options provide a satisfactory answer to this conundrum. The purchaser of a put option (like his counterpart, the call option buyer) acquires a measure of gearing to accommodate his projection of a sharply lower share price. No cash collateral is required (other than payment of the put premium), maximum profit potential is considerably increased (the underlying share price could drop to zero), and the investor's risk capital is limited to the premium paid plus expenses.

Example
   CTD share price is 69
   Three-month put with exercise price of 70 stands at 5 offered
   Investor purchases one contract (i.e. 1,000 shares) at 5.

At expiry of the option:
   (1) If the price of CTD has declined to 60, the put would have an intrinsic value of 10, i.e. double (less expenses) the original investment.
   (2) If the price of CTD remains at 69, the put would have an intrinsic value of 1.
   (3) If the price rises above 70, the put would be worthless.

The criteria involved in the selection of which strike price and over what time scale the put option is purchased should vary little from those discussed in depth in previous sections of this book. A little more attention should perhaps be given to the problem of which put option to choose, if only because the psychology of executing 'bear' positions in Stock Exchange matters is contrary to the 'normal' investment make-up of the vast majority of investors, whose natural inclination is to be bullish. The ability to sell at anywhere near the right time is one of the most difficult facets of the art of investment. Very few achieve it with any degree of consistency, and the withdrawal or elimination of private capital from equities over the past decade or two is a monument to this unfortunate 'fact'. As a result, most investors seldom hit a bear phase anywhere near the top: by the time they have decided that enough is enough in relation to their remaining, deteriorating, bull positions, the extent of the price fall has been significant enough already to take much of the steam from the bear case. In general, that is not the time to be an aggressive purchaser of put options.

Indeed, it is difficult, if not well nigh impossible, to be dogmatic about the 'rules' involved in the selection of the duration over which the put option runs. Much, of course, will depend upon the investment circumstances prevailing at the time, including how heavily over-bought the market appears to be, the imminence or otherwise of company figures, dividend declarations, etc. However, it seems likely that much of the 'action' in put options will predominate in the short-expiry series, as professional traders endeavour to capitalise upon fast-moving, short-term swings in the market. This does not imply that the longer dated option series should be ignored. Indeed, quite the opposite: they will often provide the best value among the series available to accommodate the view that share prices are due to tumble.

It is equally difficult to be too precise about the choice of exercise price for put options; the degree of pessimism felt at the point of decision will always largely determine the eventual choice. The lower the strike price (relative to the current share price), the 'cheaper' (i.e. lower priced) the put option (but the further the price has to fall before money is made by exercising the put). So, for those confident of a substantial fall in a share price from existing levels, high gearing can be achieved via the lowest strike price available. Exercise prices closer to the existing underlying share price will accommodate a less bearish interpretation of future price movement.

Two examples involving Racal and BP (Table 10.1) may highlight some of these points: in both cases the underlying share price dropped dramatically over a relatively short time scale and in so doing generated huge percentage gains in the three- and six-month at- and out-of-the-

Table 10.1

Racal	A	B	
Date	4.9.81	25.9.81	
Stock price (p)	455	377	(−17%)
Options			
Nov. 460	25	87	(+248%)
Nov. 420	10	48	(+380%)
Nov. 390	4	27	(+575%)
Options			
Feb. 460	32	88	(+175%)
Feb. 420	17	50	(+194%)
Feb. 390	8	30	(+275%)
BP	A	B	
Date	4.9.81	25.9.81	
Stock price (p)	302	256	(−15%)
Options			
Oct. 300	15	44	(+193%)
Oct. 280	6	28	(+366%)
Options			
Jan. 300	22	46	(+109%)
Jan. 280	13	32	(+146%)

money option series (i.e. where the exercise price is below the prevailing share price).

In both cases under review, the short heaviest out-of-the-money options (Racal Nov. 390 and BP Oct. 280) showed the greatest capital appreciation. However, the dramatic fall in the underlying share price required to produce such gains within the time scale of the option was exceptional. In retrospect, of course, it is always so simple! In reality, few investors anticipated such a sizeable retracement, and the marginally in-the-money series for the three- or six-month time scale would probably have seemed the more intelligent choice at the time. The resultant rewards, while clearly less startling were nevertheless most acceptable.

General 'rules' for straight put option purchases

(1) Don't buy puts *unless* the interpretation of the general market level is heavily over-bought. It is extremely difficult to make money on the bear tack in a particular stock which looks too high while the general market remains firm. It is safer to wait until the market as a whole is ripe for a set-back and then hit the stock hard. After all, if

137

your interpretation is correct, the stock should have underperformed the market during this interim stage.

(2) Don't hesitate to sell the option (i.e. close the put purchase) when a profit target has been achieved, irrespective of how much longer the option still has to run to expiry.

(3) Unless the investor is *convinced* that a share will fall significantly from current levels, purchase a put option with a strike price at or just below the current price of the stock (i.e. with little or no intrinsic value).

Put options for holders of the underlying security

For a holder or prospective holder of an underlying security, the purchase of a put option is manifestly a more satisfactory hedge against a fall in the share price than the alternative strategy of writing a covered call option. The investor, unsure of his market timing particularly in the short term, might use put options as a form of insurance policy. If the stock goes up, as he believes it will, he will benefit from his position in the underlying security and will forfeit his insurance policy (put option). If the underlying share price falls rather than rises (which he suspected it might in the near term), he may do one of two things. Firstly, he can exercise the put and, in so doing, sell the underlying shares at the exercise price or, secondly, he can sell the put, which will have increased in value as the share decline gathered pace. This choice of whether to sell the put option (to close it) or exercise it (to sell the underlying security) must inevitably depend upon the investment judgement made at the time. If the fall in the share price has unnerved the investor and shaken his faith in the bull case, he might adopt the latter strategy; if he feels it is merely a short-term retracement which will be more than made up subsequently, he might close out the put (by selling it) and leave his bull position in the underlying shares intact. Numerous permutations and combinations of strategy are available to accommodate the investment view. For example:

(1) Neutral/uncertain view – buy stock and purchase put option.

(2) Bearish view – buy put option and purchase stock after it has fallen.

(3) Bearish view but not able to sell underlying share – purchase several puts.

SELLING (WRITING) PUT OPTIONS

Just as call options are for buying and selling, the same applies to put options. As I have just explained, buyers of puts seek gearing and profits from a straightforward downward projection of the underlying share prices. Sellers of put options on the other hand (like writers of call options) may have varying motives, i.e. their aims may be less 'obvious'. This aim could be to earn premium 'income' to augment dividend income from the underlying security and thus boost the overall return on capital employed; or writing puts may be deployed to acquire additional shares at a predetermined level below the current market price. Whichever strategy is attempted, however, the writer of puts is obliged to purchase the stock from a purchaser of the option as soon as the latter decides to exercise his right to sell the stock. In other words, once a buyer of a put exercises it (and he can do so at any time up to expiry), a writer (selected by the same computerised random selection process applicable to call options) will be obliged to purchase it at the exercise price. His 'effective' price, of course, will be the exercise price of the option less the premium received from writing the option.

As with a call option, the premium of a put will be made up of intrinsic value plus time value, or just plain time value. This time value, of course, represents the amount which the buyer of a put is willing to pay over and above the intrinsic value in the expectation that the price of the underlying security will decline sufficiently to make exercise of the option a profitable proposition. Once again, as with calls, when there is no time value left in the put option, the premium will reflect intrinsic value only (i.e. the difference between the underlying share price and the exercise price). If, at expiry, the market price is above the exercise price of the put, it will have no intrinsic value and will 'waste' to zero.

The writer of a put option is obliged to purchase the stock at the exercise price if the put is exercised, as I have already pointed out. In fast-moving markets this potential liability may leave the writer exposed to a sharp drop in the share price beyond his effective purchase price (exercise price less premium receipts). Just in case readers are getting fretful that traded puts are in any way less flexible then their call counterparts in this respect (or place the writer in a position similar to that of a taker of put money in the traditional option market with all its disadvantages), let me nullify any such fears at the outset. Flexibility of manoeuvre *is* an integral part of a traded options market and always will be. The trader in puts, whether as a buyer or a seller, must have the ability to terminate his position (by a closing sale or purchase). Accordingly, the put writer can close his position by purchasing an identical option at the prevailing price at any time prior to exercise, in the same way that a writer of calls can do likewise prior to being assigned. A simple hypothetical example might be useful at this juncture to illustrate these various points.

Example

An investor decides to write a CTD Jan. 70 put (share price 70) and receives a premium of five points.

    (1) If, at expiry of the option, the CTD share price is 60, the put will be exercised and the writer obliged to purchase the shares at 70. His 'effective' purchase price, of course, is 65 (70 − 5).

    (2) If, at expiry, the CTD share price is 75, the option will be abandoned and the writer will pocket the five points.

    (3) If, within the life of the option, the share price dropped to 65, the writer (fearing a further fall in the price) might decide to buy back his option at the prevailing price: he would undoubtedly cut a small loss but he would terminate his written position and have no further potential liability.

While the maximum liability of the uncovered call writer is unlimited, the maximum loss for an uncovered put writer would occur if the value of the underlying security dropped to zero. Although this seems highly improbable bearing in mind the calibre of the underlying securities likely to list traded puts, a re-run of the conditions which persisted from 1973 to the end of 1974 would have made life distinctly uncomfortable and most unprofitable for the naked put writer. Like the uncovered writer of calls, his maximum profit is limited to the net amount received for the put, which must presumably question the risk/reward potentiality of the transaction. Incidentally, 'covered' put writing would involve being 'short' (i.e. selling shares not owned) of the underlying security on a one-for-one basis: not only is this impractical in the London market but it places the writer in a position of massive exposure on the upside. It is not to be recommended.

Institutional investors may well discover how useful a strategy writing puts can be: it is tailor-made to suit the requirements of those endeavouring to purchase selected equities on falling prices. It is thus an alternative to leaving low bids for lines of shares in the market on a dull day (trading not climatic conditions) in the hope or expectation that the price weakness will accelerate. Writing put options has one major advantage over this 'method' and ought to find favour with the more 'commercial' managers of portfolios. If the price structure of the shares does not weaken further, the low bids will not succeed and the investor will end up empty-handed. Likewise, the writer of put options will not acquire any stock by virtue of being exercised against at the strike price. So, as far as that goes, it is level pegging; but the writer of puts has, at the very least, collected some premium receipts for the written puts which subsequently expire worthless. Not a lot, perhaps, to placate his frustration, but a little is always better than nothing as his opposite number in this example will discover! ·

Numerous variations or permutations on the theme will be permitted under the rules; the dominating factor will usually be the investment decision prevailing at the time regarding the underlying security. For example, if a fairly aggressive, short-term, bearish stance is adopted, the put could be written and the position margined, in the expectation that a unit holding of the underlying security will be purchased in due course at the exercise price of the put less the premium receipts. Alternatively, part of the intended holding in the underlying security can be purchased at the current market price and a put option written with a lower exercise price. A hypothetical example will probably highlight the relevant points more clearly.

Example

An investor wishes to purchase 10,000 CTD shares, currently priced at 65. However, he is fearful of a short-term reaction in the share price and hence, while content to make a start at current levels, he really hopes to buy the balance lower down and, in so doing, improve his average purchase price. He therefore decides to:

(1) purchase 5,000 shares at 65, and
(2) write five CTD 60 puts for three points per contract.

If the share price drops below 60 at expiry, the put will be exercised, and the writer will purchase an additional 5,000 shares (five contracts) at $60 - 3 = 57$. His average price for his holding in 10,000 shares will be 65 + 57 divided by 2 = 61 (plus expenses).

If the share price remains above 60 at expiry, the option will expire worthless, and the writer will pocket the three points on five contracts (i.e. 5,000 shares). He will still own the original 5,000 shares purchased at 65, but he will have written this price down by the three premium points taken, i.e. to 62.

Margin requirements for put options

Unlike the rules for call options, the deposit of the underlying stock as collateral is not permitted for traded put options.

(1) *Written positions only*

The minimum margin requirement is based on the daily closing price of the underlying stock, and, as in the case of traded call options, is calculated at 25% of that stock price plus or minus (as appropriate) the amount by which the option series lies in- or out-of-the-money. Readers are reminded once more that an in-the-money traded put option is one where the market price is below the exercise price and accordingly margin requirements for a traded put will increase with a fall in the underlying stock price.

(2) *Spread positions*

Where an investor is both the holder and a writer of traded put options on the same stock, and the expiry date of the series held is the same as or later than the series written, the margin requirement will be calculated by reference to the difference between the two exercise prices as shown below.

(a) Where the exercise price of the series held is less than the series written, margin will be calculated by multiplying the difference between the two exercise prices by the number of shares involved on the written side.

(b) Where the exercise price of the series held is the same as or greater than the series written, no margin will be required.

11

Combining puts and calls

Finally, there are option strategies available to accommodate the investor who, by his own admission, has not the faintest idea which way a particular share might move, but is nevertheless convinced that, in the words of the old maxim, 'the only thing for certain is that the share will fluctuate.' Option strategies under the heading of straddles and combinations are tailor-made to suit such blissful indecision.

STRADDLES

A *straddle* involves the simultaneous purchase of a put option and a call option on the same share with an identical exercise price and expiry date (i.e. buying a straddle) or, alternatively, the simultaneous writing of a put and call option on the same share with an identical exercise price and expiry date (i.e. writing a straddle). *Buying a straddle* is only suitable for the investor who is convinced that the underlying share price is capable of a substantial price movement (irrespective of the direction) over the life-span of the option. The movement in the underlying share price will need to be of significant proportions one way to allow for the fact that, in backing the likelihood of a move either way, the investor has been obliged to purchase two premiums. His profit will materialise if, and only if, the movement in the share price either way generates a premium total in excess of the premium cost at the time of purchase. If the share fails to move at all over the life of the option, his maximum loss will be the cost of the two options plus expenses. Another CTD hypothetical example illustrates the point.

Example
The CTD share price stands at 70 and the investor anticipates three months' volatility. He decides to purchase a Jan. 70 call for a premium of 6, and a Jan.

70 put for a premium of 5. Accordingly, he has purchased the straddle for 11 (6 + 5 plus two sets of expenses). If the CTD share price moves outside the parameters of 59 (70 – 11) and 81 (70 + 11), the investor will profit by either exercising or selling whichever option it becomes profitable so to do. If the stock rises to 90, he will exercise or sell the call for a gain of 20 (less the premium cost of 11); profit on the transaction is thus 9 points. The same will happen in reverse if the share price slumps to 50. Total loss of the 11 points premium (plus expenses) will occur if no action is taken and the share price finishes at 70 on expiry day; at any other level between 59 and 81, part of the cost of the transaction can be recouped by either a purchase or sale of the relevant option.

Writing a straddle is the reverse of buying a straddle in every sense of the term. It will be undertaken by the investor who anticipates that the underlying share price will *not* alter substantially over the tenure of the option. The investor writing a straddle is aiming to capitalise on the additional cash flow generated from writing two premiums rather than one (i.e. the put and the call on the same underlying security, exercise price and expiry date). As the majority of shares listing options are chosen for their high volatility potentiality, the likelihood of the underlying share price moving in a very restricted price band around the srike price of the options is remote. Indeed, the risks involved in the strategy clearly outweigh the likely rewards, and any investor using this ploy must do so *only* as a holder of the underlying security. Otherwise, for the promise of a relatively insignificant maximum reward, the straddle writer is exposed to unlimited potential losses through his uncovered call and heavy potential losses through having the put exercised on him at the strike price if the share falls substantially. Either way, a financial nightmare not to be recommended too often in an era of modern extreme price volatility! Unlike the buyer of a straddle, the straddle writer requires the share to remain *inside* the premium price parameter – a rather optimistic expectation these days!

Example
The CTD share price is 70. A Jan. 70 put is written at 3 and a Jan. 70 call is written at 4. Total premium 'income' is 7 less expenses: the profit parameters for the writer lie *within* the 63–77 band.

I have stressed that in no circumstances should the inexperienced option trader 'dabble' in written straddles without the cover of the underlying shares. In writing a straddle he is thus taking one of two basic decisions regarding his underlying shareholding.

(1) If the call option is exercised against him (at the strike price), he

is acquiescing to a sale of the underlying security at the strike price plus the total premium receipts from both the written call and the written put.

(2) If this does not happen, the likelihood is that the put will be exercised against him at the strike price, and he will be obliged to purchase additional shares at the strike price less the total premium receipts from the written call and the written put.

If the investor is unhappy with either one of these two potential results, he should not write the straddle.

COMBINATIONS

The same 'rules' and criteria just discussed for straddles apply equally to writers of *combinations*: the only difference in this transaction will be in the 'mix', i.e. a combination of puts and calls using different exercise prices and/or different expiry dates. The three hypothetical CTD combinations below illustrate the point.

CTD Jan. 70 put }
CTD Jan. 80 call } *or*   CTD Jan. 70 put }
CTD Apr. 70 call } *or*   CTD Jan. 80 put }
CTD Apr. 80 call }

While the 'structural' difference between straddles and combinations will obviously alter the risk/reward parameter of the transaction, the same 'background' conditions are necessary for a written combination to end up being profitable, i.e. low volatility and a tight trading range. The choice of put and call combination will be wide and variable; once again, it will reflect largely the investment case and the market judgement for the share price over the option life, and this judgement will determine the extent of the rewards likely and the level of risk tolerance.

Margin requirements for combinations

Where an investor has a written position in traded call and traded put options on the same underlying stock, margin may be calculated at 25% of the underlying stock price (one side only) plus the amount by which one or both contracts, as appropriate, lie(s) in-the-money. Out-of-the-money contracts will not be taken into account when computing the margin requirements for combinations.

This combination concession need not be applied where by margining each position independently a lower margin will result.

Examples

(1) *In-the-money put and in-the-money call*
Margin is 25% of the underlying stock price (one side only) plus the in-the-money element for the put, plus the in-the-money element for the call.

(2) *In-the-money put and out-of-the-money call*
Margin is 25% of the underlying stock price (one side only) plus the in-the-money element for the put.

(3) *In-the-money call and out-of-the-money put*
Margin is 25% of the underlying stock price (one side only) plus the in-the-money element for the call.

(4) *Both contracts out-of-the-money*
Margin is 25% of the underlying stock price (one side only).

Glossary

Abandon: To allow an option to expire without exercising it.

Assignment notice: Formal notification from the London Options Clearing House to a writer requiring him to fulfil his contractual obligation to buy or sell the underlying security.

At-the-money: The underlying share price stands at the same price as the exercise price.

Board dealer: A firm appointed by the Council of the Stock Exchange to be responsible for the custody and execution of public limit orders and for ensuring the orderly conduct of trading in a particular option class.

Call option: A call option contract confers the right to buy a fixed number of shares at a specified price within a predetermined period of time.

Certificateless trading: Options are a form of certificateless trading because the Clearing Corporation will not issue certificates to prove an option's ownership. Evidence of ownership is found in the broker's books and the client's contract note.

Checking: The checking of all option contracts by parties to match bought and written contracts.

Class: All option contracts covering the same underlying security.

Clearing firms/members: Firms engaged in clearing option contracts for themselves or other members or public member firms and accepting responsibility *vis-à-vis* the Clearing Corporation for the bargains.

Closing purchase transaction: A transaction in which a writer (seller) buys back an option identical to one which he has written, thus extinguishing his liability as a writer.

Closing sale transaction: A transaction in which the holder of an option disposes of it in the market to another buyer.

Contract: An option issued by the Clearing Corporation which, in the main, will relate to 1,000 shares of the underlying security in London.

Cover: Underlying stock pledged to LOCH as collateral for a written option.

Covered writer: The writer of a call option who pledges to LOCH the underlying security.

Covered: The writer holds all the underlying securities for the option written.

Credit: A positive balance resulting from an opening spread transaction.

Crowd: The market makers and market agents at a particular dealing pitch.

Dealing pitch: The pitch where one or more classes of options are traded.

Debit: Negative balance resulting from an opening spread transaction.

Exercise notice: A formal notification to LOCH that the holder of an option wishes to exercise it by buying or selling the underlying stock.

Exercise price/Strike price: The specific price per share at which the underlying security may be purchased upon exercise of the option contract.

Expiry date: The date on which an option contract expires.

Horizontal spread/Calendar spread/Time spread: A spread between two options (i.e. one bought and one written) on the same underlying security, having the same exercise price but different expirations.

In-the-money option: A call option whose exercise price is below the current market price of the underlying security, or a put option whose exercise price is above the current market price of the underlying security.

148

Intrinsic value: A call option has intrinsic value if the exercise price of the option is lower than the price of the underlying security. A put option has intrinsic value if the exercise price of the option is higher than the price of the underlying security. In each case, the intrinsic value is the difference between the exercise price and the price of the underlying security.

London Options Clearing House (LOCH): A wholly owned subsidiary company of the Stock Exchange responsible for the registration and settlement of all traded option transactions.

Margin: The sum required as collateral from writers of London traded options who are not covered by the lodgement of the underlying securities.

Market maker: A jobber or broker who, under the rules of the Stock Exchange, is permitted to make a market, as principal, in traded options.

Open interest: The number of option contracts outstanding at any time, either in a particular class or in all classes.

Opening purchase: A transaction in which the buyer becomes the holder of an option.

Opening sale: A transaction in which the seller assumes liability for the performance of an option contract, thereby becoming the writer of that contract.

Option class: All options of the same type pertaining to the same underlying security. Calls and puts comprise separate classes.

Option series: All options of the same class having the same exercise price and expiry date.

Out-of-the-money option: A call option whose exercise price is above the current price of the underlying security, or a put option whose exercise price is below the current price of the underlying security.

Premium: The price of an option agreed upon by the buyer and seller. The premium is paid by the buyer to the seller.

Put option: A put option contract confers the right to sell a fixed number of shares at a specified price within a predetermined period of time.

Spread: The purchase and sale of different series of options in the same class by the same principal.

Spread margin: The margin required for an open uncovered sale which is offset by an opening purchase of contracts of a different series in the same class by the same principal.

Time value: That part of the option premium which reflects the remaining life of an option. The longer the time remaining before expiry, the higher the time value will tend to be.

Uncovered writer: A writer who does not own the underlying shares upon which the option is sold. Also referred to as *Naked writer*.

Underlying security: A stock in respect of which an option contract has been bought or sold (written).

Unit of trading or contract: The number of shares of the underlying stock designated by the Stock Exchange as the subject of a single option contract.

Vertical price spread: A spread involving the purchase and sale of options of the same class having common expiration dates but different exercise prices.

Writer: The seller of an option contract.

Index